Musical Chairs

The ups and downs of the music world and other short stories.
An autobiographical diary of my life.

by
Sir Andrew Jay Stimmel

Published by Andrew Jay

ISBN 978-0-578-94596-5 (hardback)

Library of Congress Control Number: 2021913832

United States Copyright Office
Registration Number TXu 2-269-507
Effective Date of Registration: July 16, 2021

Published by Andrew Jay
Palm Desert, California

Author: Sir Andrew Jay Stimmel

Editors: Eduardo Santiago and Lynn Jones Green

Cover Illustrations by Josh Kirby

Cover/interior design and layout:
Mark E. Anderson, www.aquazebra.com

AquaZebra™
Web, Book & Print Design

Printed in the United States of America

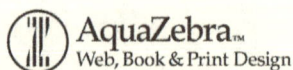

Foreword

If you work in the entertainment industry long enough, your roots grow, associations multiply and your stories become more and more entertaining. Suddenly, you're connected to nearly everyone of historical value or significance.

Such has been the case for my friend, colleague and mentor, Andrew "Ajay" Stimmel, who started out as a professional musician some 45 years ago and ultimately flourished in music distribution, where he enjoyed a successful career and reputation latter part due primarily to the countless stories he could offer up to clients and colleagues alike.

Ajay always seemed to be in the right place at the right time, rubbing elbows with an illustrious panoply of pop culture personalities. If a conversation turned to rock music, actors, artists, and Ajay was within earshot, there was usually a good chance he had met with, jammed with, partied with or slept with the topic of conversation.

I used to encourage him to write down every brush with history and culture he ever had, never thinking he'd find the time or patience to collect his memories, mementos and musings into one cohesive document.

But here we are.

I present to you the life of Andrew J. Stimmel one of the most colorful people I've had the pleasure of calling a friend in my lifetime. He is a cultural conundrum: A rock 'n' roll legend that history won't record or remember, and yet no one who has met him ever forgets him.

Welcome, my friends, to the Cult of Ajay.

John Bowen

Capitol Records	EMI Music
Former VP Sales	Former VP Sales
Los Angeles, California	Los Angeles, California

Dedication

This book is dedicated to:

- My dear mother and father, who always encouraged me to follow my path, whatever I chose.

- My brother Kenny and my sister Jackie who only remember so much of my whacky journey in my personal life nevertheless, they urged me to write this book.

- My nephew Simon Journey, whose appreciation of music is second to none, and his papa, Doug Journey.

- My Grandma Rae Kulander; if it wasn't for her my love for music would never have started in the first place.

- Grandpa Sam Kulander, my pal as a youngster. He introduced me to the coolest restaurants in town growing up.

- My dear Grandpa Jack and Grandma Bessie who took care of me as a toddler while my mom and dad were at work.

I have many friends, family and musicians that I need to dedicate this book to So, in no special order here we go! Steve and Barbara Kessler; Aunt Janis and Uncle Joe, Aunt Isabel and Uncle Joel, Lynne Tasman/Jack Wasserman, Brian Tasman, Ronni, Jody, Uncle Lowell and Barbara Sigmund, Logan, Lucas, Vanessa Stimmel, Amy Stein, Alan Weitz, Andy C. Doback, Ford and Vicki Kaufholz, John Bowen, Michael Wittman, Steven Hoffman, David Paul Federbush, Randy Jay Blitz, Steve Donahue, Leslie Hollas and Peter, David Ewing, Terry Reid, Chelsea Rae King, Charlie Brand, Arturo Vega and The Ramones, James Sliman and The Dead Boys, Arthur Killer Kane, The New York Dolls, Frank and Gail Zappa, The Runaways (Jackie, Lita, Cherie, Joan and Sandy) Spencer Hirsch, Tony Vick, Vince Lara and Victor Angel Rivas, Ethel Greenwald Epstein, Hy Golding, Terry Melcher, Ray Manzarek, Todd Rundgren, Jim Capaldi, Jeff Healey, Steve Brownlee, Gina Zamparelli, Andrew Gold, Chris" Skippy" Rogowski, Dane Michael Peterson, Craig K. Hayes,

Joey Altruda, Elliot Kendall, Christopher Turnbow, Dave James, Kevin Ware and Jimmy Sena.

Table of Contents

Introduction

Dear Readers,

I have tried to make my life story entertaining and enlightening, including the many trials and tribulations I have had. This is my first attempt at writing a book, which initially began about a decade ago due to friends telling me they always enjoyed the stories of my colorful life in the music business and beyond.

I'm hoping reading my autobiography will be an enjoyable experience for you.

—Andrew J. Stimmel

Chapter One
Childhood Years 1950's

My life began at 10:00 pm July 25th 1955, at New York Hospital Manhattan, New York.

When I was born, I made funny sounds. So many that my parents and relatives called me Gerald McBoing Boing, a popular cartoon character in the early 1950's who speaks through sound effects instead of words. The original story was from Dr. Seuss. It's no wonder I've had a fascination with his works to this day. Now that I'm thinking about it, I can't remember when I finally did speak.

In my early youth, our family lived in an apartment in Brooklyn. Ever since I can remember, there was always music playing at home. My grandma played piano and sang. She performed at many events through the years. When I was three years old, she sat me up on her piano stool to tutor me, but I was not a very good student. I drew cartoon faces on the musical notes she wrote. Nevertheless, my love for music was born.

Grandma and Grandpa had a really neat RCA Victor console cabinet with a turntable on top, and slots below to store records. It was beautifully made in red-brownish mahogany wood and it sounded amazing in hi-fi. Their apartment was on the second floor of the building located at 73-37 Austin Street in Forest Hills. The structure was built in 1928, and was nine stories high containing eighty-six units. It was an old art deco building and the style was reflected in the vintage hardware in both of their bathrooms. The ceramic tile flooring was black and white. Even the elevator in their building was a work of art. I remember the beautiful brass hardware and the heavy gate you had to close manually. The buttons for each floor lit up when you pressed them. Looking out of their living room windows, I could see and hear trains on the Long Island Railroad which would pass through during the day.

Grandma loved Liberace and Wayne Newton, while Grandpa was more of a big band fan. He was a pharmacist and purchased his first drug store in 1926. It was on Ave A at the corner of 2nd Street in Lower Manhattan's Greenwich Village.

By the time I came along, he had sold the pharmacy. Unfortunately, one horrible incident prompted that decision. He was robbed and beaten so badly by some random hoodlum that he was in the hospital for a long while. He never ever talked about that day. I found out the whole story from my grandma one afternoon while she was cooking her famous pan-fried hamburgers on the stove.

Grandma was the best cook! Awesome matzo ball soup with chicken, carrots, dill and other special ingredients. I can still taste that broth. Her roast beef brisket was another of her specialties, and even the grilled Velveeta cheese sandwiches she made for my brother and me were delicious.

When our family visited on the weekends, my grandpa and I used to walk together on Austin Street to get fresh bagels and lots of other goodies for brunch. There was a local diner nearby that had a model train revolving around the counter with blinking lights and it choo -chooed as it carried your food out of the kitchen to where you were sitting. The diner was called The Hamburger Train, and it originally opened in 1954. It was located on Queens Blvd above the 63rd Street subway stop. One time I went to grab my hamburger off the electric train but missed as it went by too fast. Grandpa told me "Don't worry; it'll come back around again." Those restaurants of the past sure were lots of fun when I was growing up.

At home, my parents played exotica records such as Martin Denny, Les Baxter and Yma Sumac. Little did I know there would be a bygone era coming back to life decades later! A Tiki lounge exotica resurgence! I found several photos of my parents at the

Ronjo Hotel in Montauk in the 1960's.

The Ronjo was recognized as a luxury hotel complete with a namesake Tiki god to welcome and maybe protect the guests. It was situated a block away from the Atlantic Ocean. The Rolling Stones hung out there with Andy Warhol who (from what I've been told) owned a beautiful beach house nearby. I'm sure my mom and dad were drinking plenty of Mai Tai's and other exotic cocktails back then at The Ronjo. They stayed over for a weekend for fun in the sun while us kids stayed at our grandparents.

My parents listened to big bands, jazz, soundtracks and vocalists such as Frank Sinatra, whom my mother adored. Many years later, my mother told me that she and her sister, Janis, skipped school to see Frank Sinatra live at the Paramount Theatre near Times Square. This was in the 1940's when teenagers were called Bobbysoxers. Wow! I wonder if my grandma ever knew.

When my brother, Kenny, was born a few years after me, many adventures were about to take place. The 1950's was a great time for music and a great time to be alive. It marked the birth of rock 'n' roll! An abundance of songs from that decade are today, staple classics that will live on forever to eternity! From rock to jazz, great music kept on coming.

Mom and Dad bought a little portable record player for me and my brother to listen to our 45's of children's music from Disney and Golden Records. The vinyl discs came in bright colors, mostly red, yellow, and orange. My brother and I laughed a lot as many recordings were pretty silly. Disney recordings however, told stories with more sophisticated music and in a more dramatic style.

Mom and Dad took me and Kenny on trips to Coney Island, Atlantic City, Jones Beach, The New York World's Fair, The Metropolitan Museum of Art, apple picking, and visiting the Hershey Chocolate Factory in Hershey, Pennsylvania. Oh, one quick note: When we went on that Hershey tour, I remember Kenny wanted to climb right into the transparent thick glass containing ocean waves of chocolate. That whole scene reminded me of Willy Wonka's chocolate factory movie from 1971. I'll have to admit, the heavy scent of that deep chocolate was intoxicating, especially for my brother and me.

Just like most kids in America in the 1950's, we played with toys and built funny things with alphabet blocks, Lincoln logs, and Tinker toys. We also loved Play-Doh. We made some crazy creatures out of that goofy colored stuff. It was fun at the time. Once, Kenny tried to eat that Play-Doh, but he spit it out, saying it tasted too salty. To this day, I truly believe he was really going to eat that stuff. Silly Putty was also fun to play with unless you tried to eat it or rub it on your head. One time it got stuck in my hair. It was hard getting it out so my mother came to the rescue and carefully got it out, but she had to cut part of my hair. Slinky was silly. We would wait to see how many steps it could drop down before it stopped. We had many playsets from Disney and Hanna-Barbera that included plastic figurines. Colorforms were fun and we had many sets, from Mickey Mouse to Popeye. Colorforms were shapes and forms cut from colored vinyl that would stick to a smooth backing surface without adhesives.

When we got a little older, we played with G.I. Joe's. My friend and I had quite the imagination. We tried to create real-life war scenes by bringing them outdoors in the dirt. I'd throw G.I. Joe up against a tree; I'd pose him hanging from a branch; I put him through all sorts of nutty stuff.

One of my friends had a BB gun that shot out metal pellets. We used to shoot at these scary looking water rats down below the Whitestone Bridge.

My friends and I also had cap gun pistols that would make a cool, loud noise. You simply placed a roll of caps inside the pistol and when pulling the trigger, it would give off a loud pop crackle sound. No real bullets obviously. They were so realistic if seen from a distance! Most toys we played with were made by the Louis Marx Company, at that time the largest toy manufacturer in the world.

I loved costumes and used to dress up as Zorro, Popeye, and Davy Crockett. My brother did too. We had many costumes to choose from. We sure had fun growing up and watched most of the kid's TV programming such as Captain Kangaroo, Howdy Doody, Mickey Mouse Club, Romper Room and Wonderama.

Once, my brother and I were on live television for the taping of Wonderama with host, Sonny Fox. It was a children's television program that aired on WNEW TV in New York City from 1955 to 1977. During the show, the audience was asked if anyone would like to come up and participate in the magic trick of the day. I raised my hand like everyone else, but I also yelled really loud! Well, Sonny picked me. After the magic trick was over, I ran back up to my seat. But the funny thing was that Sonny wanted to ask me for my name. All my friends asked me why I ran away and laughed as they watched the show live on television at home.

"It wasn't as fun as I thought it would be," I told them. What I didn't say was that the studio lights were so hot that afternoon that a cupcake I was carrying melted in my hands, my shirt and my pants. I was a real mess! Each kid in the audience had received a Drake's Cake, Devil Dogs, some Ring Dings, and Yodels, in addition to other fun stuff.

Chapter Two
Teenage Years 1960's

In the 1960's, TV shows continued and in great abundance. My favorites, in no special order, were *Dobie Gillis, Leave It To Beaver, My Three Sons, Batman, The Monkees, The Munsters, The Addams Family, The Adventures of Ozzie and Harriet, The Donna Reed Show, Wonderful World of Disney, The Ed Sullivan Show, Make Room for Daddy, The Lucy Show, Time Tunnel, Lost in Space, The Twilight Zone, The Outer Limits, Superman, Looney Tunes, The Flintstones, The Jetsons,* and *Rocky & Bullwinkle.* Back then the television shows were endless. Later in the evening my dad and I would watch *The Honeymooners* together and sometimes even *Playboy After Dark!*

There were many more shows, but these were pretty much the most popular ones. Dad would bring my brother and me to baseball games at Shea Stadium to see the N.Y. Mets and Yankee Stadium to see the New York Yankees. We'd have a blast whether our teams won or not. All we needed were hot dogs, hamburgers, peanuts and a Yoo Hoo chocolate drink and we were happy as can be.

While we're on the subject of baseball, Kenny and I played in a Little League, which was sponsored by a local bank in our neighborhood, Queens County Federal Savings. I played centerfield and Kenny was a pitcher. He was lefthanded and struck out a lot of kids. He was awesome. His pitches were so fierce that many batters were afraid of him, and being lefthanded, he confused them as well. As for me, in our last game of the season, I hit a grand slam and our team won the game! After the game was over my manager handed me the baseball that all the kids on my team signed. Damn, wish I still had that ball. All that's left from those days are several photos that are stored away for memories' sake.

Dad took 8mm movies and always brought his camera wherever we traveled. My parents moved us to Whitestone, Queens, at that time. We lived in an apartment building called Cryder's Point on Powell's Cove Blvd. I'll never forget the day my parents purchased our first color television. Boy oh boy! My brother and I were glued to television more than ever. We'd watch Beatles cartoons every Saturday morning without fail. We laughed so hard because their voices were just as goofy as the storyline. Obviously, not the real Beatles voices because of copyright restrictions, but close enough for me.

During the week, after school, me and my friends used to play Stickball. It was a street game, kind of like baseball, but instead of using a bat, we would use a broomstick or wooden mop handle and hit a rubber ball like a Pensie Pinkie. It was a back-east type of game. We broke a bunch of windows in the apartment buildings nearby and got in a heck of a lot of trouble. But eventually, it all blew over with each parent chipping in a couple of bucks for new glass.

Afterwards, when our stickball games were over, we would wait for the Good Humor ice cream truck to come by. Chocolate Éclair, Toasted Almond, Strawberry Shortcake, Cookies and Cream and assorted ice cream cones were just some of our favorite flavors. Really miss those days.

Every Sunday, our family would visit my grandparents. After dinner, we'd all watch The Ed Sullivan Show together. Grandpa sat next to me and my brother. From Topo Gigio, the ever-popular Italian mouse puppet, to notable comedians of the day and outstanding musical acts such as The Beatles, The Rolling Stones, and The Dave Clark Five, it was something we looked forward to each and every weekend.

When my sister was born in 1963, things got to be even more fun! We honestly had a happy childhood full of music, art, sports, travel and more. Our parents would take us out every so often for a family dinner. We had a favorite Chinese restaurant, Gum Kew, in our neighborhood that I'll never forget. Kam Fong was another Chinese restaurant we really enjoyed.

What fascinated me beyond the food being phenomenal was their décor, especially in the bar area. It was beautifully detailed and had a Polynesian Tiki Hawaiian ambience. Netted, colored glass floats hung down from the ceiling, and the tropical cocktails were garnished with fruit kabobs and paper parasols. The bar was dimly lit and had a waterfall. Tiki statues surrounded the revolving bar. In the 1960's many Chinese restaurants had cocktail lounges that were similar, including bamboo and thatch. I remember looking at the cool, laminated cocktail menu wondering what those drinks tasted like. Some of the names scared the heck out of me when looking at the pictures: Cobra's Fang, Zombie Punch, Shark's Tooth and Scorpion Bowl. Funny, as I got older, I tried out some of those exotic cocktails, and *wow*, were they potent!

Through the years, Kenny and I collected baseball cards and comic books. We read *Mad* magazine too, but didn't understand certain things till we got older.

When I turned twelve, I told my dad I wanted to play the guitar. He said, "If you'll take guitar lessons, I'll buy you a guitar."

So, lo and behold, my first guitar was a hollow body Harmony Natural Sunburst Acoustic guitar. It sounded pretty good. But, after a while I got bored with guitar lessons. From then on, I listened to many records and tried to emulate the notes and sounds from my favorite bands at the time. Sometimes I figured out certain chords and notes, but I needed more help. So, since I knew how to read music (well, sort of) Mom and Dad purchased sheet music from many of my favorite music artists.

Kenny wanted to play the guitar also. He had played a nylon stringed acoustic guitar for a little while but later gave it up. When he did play, though, we used to write songs together and play in the bathroom because it created this cool echo sound that we found by accident. My brother's friend, Buddy played drums, but we couldn't fit a real drum set in the bathroom, so we used my mother's vinyl, padded chairs to get this real cool sound without a snare drum or floor tom. We also used my mom's old metal pans to replace real cymbals. My mom got mad and yelled at us, wondering where her two chairs had disappeared to. Yes, it was utterly ridiculous, but we had this crazy way of playing music.

This was the beginning of a taste of things to come later on. Even my little sister Jackie, wanted to play music. She started taking piano lessons, but she gave it up after a while to do other stuff. At one point, she took ballet lessons. But, several months later, she didn't want to go anymore and simply stated, "I don't want to go because I hate ballet!" Kenny and I wrote a song about that and we all laughed together afterwards.

My sister was a funny kid. One day, Kenny and I heard her crying, so we ran outside to our terrace where we spotted her head stuck in the middle of two metal bars. It was nuts! Thankfully, our mom was home and phoned the Fire Department, who handled things very well. First, they calmed my sister down. She was really scared. Then, they had to saw off one of the metal bars. When the job was done, Voila! She was set free.

We then all asked her, "Jackie, what were you trying to do anyway?" It just didn't make any sense to us. She refused to tell us. In all, we sure were glad that incident was over with and she was okay.

As time went on, Dad knew my brother and I loved music. He bought us a little stereo with turntable by a company called Lloyd's. It sounded okay; we were just kids. What did we really know about good audio sound? We were just happy to hear music in Stereo. Eventually he came around, and in late 1963 he upgraded and bought us a Panasonic Stereo with a cassette deck. At that time, we started collecting records and cassette tapes. We never liked 8track tapes. We thought they were bulky and an idiotic format.

Mom and Dad gave us an allowance. We saved what we could to buy more music, even if our parents bought our favorite records from time to time.

Right around this time, I really wanted an electric guitar.

Eventually, Dad bought me my first electric guitar. I was fifteen years old, and boy, was I excited! It was a Univox Cherry Sunburst hollow body guitar with a Univox Amplifier and a Uniwah wah wah pedal! By now, my record collection was growing at a fast pace. I'd play my records then plug in my guitar to the amplifier and play along with as much as I could.

One day, I tripped over my guitar cord and bumped into my amplifier with my reverb unit on, almost knocking it over. But what happened was this crazy sound that I had heard before. It was on a Ten Years After record called *Ssssh* and the beginning intro to the song, "Good Morning Little School Girl." Wow, it was crazy.

"Cut out the damn noise," I remember my mom yelled. I could not believe I had replicated that same sound. Man, I had to find out what other gadgets these guitar players were using.

Well, my friend Joey, who lived nearby, was an awesome guitarist. He was older than me and played in a local band. He had all these cool accessories, such as a Maestro Echoplex with these weird tape reels that had some crazy sounds and a Gibson Maestro Fuzz Tone Box. When he played "Taxman" by The Beatles, he replicated note by note George Harrison's guitar licks. Right then, my whole world of music opened up with amazing new sounds. I was hooked!

In junior high school I had a bunch of friends. A few of them played instruments like I did. We once played at our school's talent show. While playing my Univox electric guitar, suddenly, out of nowhere my guitar strap snapped, and my guitar dropped to the ground. At first, the audience thought it was part of the act, but then they laughed. I was really embarrassed but picked it up and kept playing till we finished our song. What I really wanted to do, though, was smash my guitar up like Jimi Hendrix and Pete Townsend (from The Who) used to do on stage. I remembered watching videos of them doing that very thing on television. Well, we didn't win the contest, but I didn't care. I continued playing, learning, rehearsing, and enjoying all of it.

I met more musicians in junior high school, and I got to be

friends with them. One fellow I will never forget. We played handball and basketball in the schoolyard together and hung out. He was a Turkish dude named Sinan and he played the guitar. He had a Fender Stratocaster and Vox amplifier. We used to jam together at his apartment after school. He was an incredible musician. I couldn't believe how he knew all these crazy complicated guitar licks just like many well-known rock guitarists that we both listened to at the time.

"Think you can teach me to do all that?" I asked him.

"Sure," he said in his matter-of-fact way. I was amazed that someone only two years older than me was so accomplished.

One day after school, I went to visit him. I rang the doorbell and his sister answered. She knew who I was, but she had this look on her face that something dramatically wrong had happened. I was kind of scared. She told me Sinan had killed himself.

"He jumped off the second floor of our building," she said, her voice sad but steady, as if she'd already said this too many times and was getting used to the taste of it on her tongue.

I couldn't move. I thought, *this can't be?*

"I'm sorry," she said and closed the door.

I walked home in shock thinking, *Well, he smoked cigarettes, maybe it was drugs?* I was confused and could feel the tears stinging my eyes. I still think about him every so often, whenever I hear the songs, he mastered. Why did this happen? Sinan taught me as much as I possibly could absorb about playing guitar. I'm very grateful for the time we had shared together, and I'm glad we were friends. Still, there was something like a cloud in my mind, an unsolved mystery mixed in with sadness and frustration. Little did I know at the time that the biggest loss of my young life was still ahead.

♪♫♪

Sinan was gone. I couldn't undo that. I had to focus on my other musician friends that played drums, bass, guitar and keyboards. By this time, I'd grown out of that Univox guitar, so I begged my father for a Gibson Les Paul. He knew my passion for music was serious and he told me, "We'll go together to a music shop soon, okay? Just be patient." What choice did I have?

When my father traveled on business, he always brought home a present for my brother and me. On one occasion, he brought home a record by Albert King, *"Live Wire /Blues Power"* then told me his friend had told him, "Your son needs to hear this record!" Whoever that friend was, that LP is still a valuable part of my record collection.

Several weeks later we drove to Sam Ash Music. After drooling over some of the most spectacular guitars I'd ever seen in my life, all I could do was hope for the best. To make a long story short, I came home with a 1970 Gibson SG electric, solid body, dual cutaway guitar, in a glossy walnut finish with two humbucking pickups and a Maestro Vibrola whammy bar with a nice gold velvet case. The amplifier was a Traynor Tube two-piece combo amplifier.

Living in an apartment building, it was impossible to play loud. Our next-door neighbors would no doubt complain, which they did constantly. The doorman on duty would ring our bell and warn us all the time. On the second floor above us, the fucking annoying neighbors would bang hard on their floor on our ceiling, making their point clear.

So, with that said, I purchased a set of headphones for times when needed. Ended up with Koss Pro 4AA Studio headphones that sounded pretty good and served their purpose. My brother and I would both share together listening to records. As time went on, I joined a band with a great bunch of local musician friends, that played drums, bass, organ and guitar.

We jammed a lot at the keyboard player's home. His mom and dad let us practice in their basement downstairs. The acoustics weren't so good and we were a bit cramped, but we were all glad we could play somewhere without other people bothering us.

Our keyboard player had a great big Hammond organ and a big Leslie speaker that had this full, deep rich sound. The bass player had a Cherry Red Gibson EB3 and the drummer played on a beautiful blue sparkled Ludwig full set. My Gibson sounded great and matched up well with the band. Later, another guitar player was added. He played a Gibson Black Beauty Les Paul that sounded incredible.

After rehearsing for a while, we started sounding better and played at a summer pool party in a community of apartment buildings near where I lived in Whitestone. We had a few other odd jobs such as playing at a Bar Mitzvah. We made no money; we were just having fun.

Our drummer told us that we could practice any time at his parents' place, so we brought our equipment over there and were able to practice quite often during the week. It was awfully loud in that basement, so we tried to make the acoustics better by placing egg cartons and all sorts of materials on the basement walls. It worked well and softened up the sound.

As time went by, I took my guitar over one late Friday afternoon to our drummer's house. His older sister answered the door.

"Is Dean home?" I asked. "We have band practice."

Déjà vu; just like before, an unthinkable tragedy. Dean supposedly was struck on the head while heavily messed up on methaqualone Quaaludes at some party.

"All the other boys have already picked up their instruments," she said. "Do you have anything stored here?"

"Just my amplifier," I replied. It was too big and heavy to carry home, so I picked it up the following week. I was just too upset to go any sooner. I couldn't believe this had happened again, to another musician friend. I found out later that it was indeed an overdose. At first, I was thinking maybe this was brought about after breaking up with his girlfriend. The other band members were also in shock. We couldn't fathom just like that, he was gone.

With heavy hearts we found another drummer and continued to play a whole bunch of popular songs, not really any originals. We had many jam sessions, but never performed anywhere else again.

♪♫♪

So, here we are December 31st, 1969. I was only fourteen

years old and asked my parents if I could go to The Fillmore East to see Jimi Hendrix and his Band of Gypsys with my friends for a special show on New Year's Eve. It was a Thursday night. There were two shows, one at 8:00 p.m. and the other at 11:30 p.m. The performances were going to be recorded for an album on Capitol Records. It would be their first time playing together as a powerhouse trio. Jimi Hendrix, Buddy Miles and Billy Cox. Both my parents said, "Absolutely Not! Drugs will be there, and it's not safe!"

After throwing a temper tantrum, I understood. I was upset, but knew deep down they were just looking out for my wellbeing. So, I kept my original Fillmore flyer handbill and stored it in a box with my other rock 'n' roll memorabilia. Tickets to that concert were only $5.00 & better seats were available for $7.00 at the Fillmore ticket booth.

I picked up the Vinyl LP on the day of release. It was an historical night. I just had to move on and not fret about not going to that show. An interesting fact is that the album was the only recording Hendrix made on Capitol Records. He recorded on Reprise throughout the rest of his career.

Chapter Three
Rock 'n' Roll Years 1970's

In 1972, my parents moved me, my brother, and my sister to Ann Arbor, Michigan. My dad had a once in a lifetime sales opportunity in his business of selling women's apparel. He traveled more than ever before, but got paid a higher salary to support our family. I ranted and raved and did not want to move. I wanted to stay in New York. I had many friends and knew I would get to play in a cool rock band sooner or later.

My dad asked me, "Do you have a job? Where are you going to live?"

"With my friends or at Grandma and Grandpa's, I told him.

He said, "You're seventeen years old! C'mon, get in the car. You'll be okay, and you can always visit."

So, it turned out that Dad had purchased a four-bedroom house with a large backyard from the principal of a local high school in Ann Arbor. It was located not far from downtown. My brother, my sister and I each had our own bedroom. It even had a large basement with another small room and private bathroom. I painted my room purple and hung up all my rock posters. I played music in the basement and was so happy to play loud with no neighbors complaining. It was so cool. The family piano was down there also.

We wanted to have a dog, so our parents brought home a cocker spaniel /fox terrier mix puppy. We called him Ringo. He was a cool pup but was quite mischievous. On one occasion, my mother had a PTA Meeting at the house and Ringo was trying to hump this woman's leg. She screamed! So, my brother pulled him away. Another time, while walking our dog, a nice couple said, "What a cute dog. What's his name?" They gently petted him, then he decided to pee on the husband's leg. We eventually had to give this little stinker up as he turned out to be quite a menace.

I finished up high school in Ann Arbor, but while in school, I met a whole bunch of talented musicians. One of the friends I made played bass guitar. His name was Aaron. He said we could play music on the weekends at his parents' house. So, I brought my guitar over one Saturday afternoon. I had already sold my amplifier beforehand, but he told me he had a few amplifiers at home.

When I saw Aaron's vintage tweed Fender Bassman and Fender champ amplifiers, I flipped! These old tube amplifiers were from the 1950's and in remarkable shape. What a great sound they had! We jammed after school and played a bunch of blues tunes. There was a great big blues rock scene going on in Ann Arbor at that time. Aaron had two friends who were collectors of vintage Fender and Gibson amplifiers and guitars. They traveled all over the United States in search of vintage equipment from newspaper ads and magazines, such as the *Recycler*. I didn't know where their money was coming from, but I figured they must have bought merchandise for a very reasonable price and sold it for a huge profit.

One day, Aaron and I drove over to their home to say hello and check things out. When we were walking through their hallway, I froze. I could not believe what I saw! Stacks of 1950's Fender Tweed amplifiers all lined up in this large room. Practically Every model was on display. While hanging out with these guys, Jay and Tom, I spotted a little 1958 Fender Deluxe amplifier with one Jensen speaker; and asked if I could plug my guitar in. When I heard that smooth, rich tone and sustained feedback at full volume, I was immediately sold. My guitar sounded absolutely amazing!

"All these vintage tube amps sound great," Jay told me.

"How much are you asking?"

He told me $100.00. Well, you can imagine the rest of this story. Best little amplifier I ever owned. It was also the ninety-eighth model made by Fender. Today's worth, you ask? In the thousands. So, it took a little while for me to get adjusted to the lifestyle in Ann Arbor, Michigan.

True to his word, my father helped pay for a few trips back to New York so I could see my friends. We'd take the train to Greenwich Village. Just like we had done in old times, we took the train downtown and went vinyl record hunting. Back in the day, we used to grab a copy or two of Robert Crumb's Zap Comix and purchase other underground comics. This was in the late 1960's with blacklight posters, psychedelic and rock posters that were hung up on the walls of several different headshops in the area.

So many cool posters were available, it was honestly hard to choose. Some posters were even tacked up to the ceiling of some of these shops. I remember picking up two awesome Jimi Hendrix posters. One was a black-light poster and the other was a group shot of the whole band taken from the back cover of an Electric Ladyland album. Another poster I picked up was of Frank Zappa's *Phi Zappa Krappa*; it was a picture of Frank sitting on a toilet seat. Man, just wish I could have saved some of those vintage posters, but I did save all my Zap Comics, rock magazines, and records.

We walked many blocks and stopped to eat at good ole Ray's Pizza on 8th Street for a couple of slices with soda. Tasted just as good as I could remember. Since Electric Ladyland Studios was located nearby, we just had to stop by in hopes of maybe seeing someone famous. It was located at 52nd West 8th Street. We rang the bell, and an attendant came out to greet us.

"You guys have an appointment?"

We were kind of nervous, but asked if we could take a quick tour.

He said, "Here's our card. Call back at another time and maybe we can arrange a little tour for you guys if we're not too busy."

Well, at least this dude was polite and nice to us. Funny thing, I still have that card he gave me.

One of the record shops we needed to see, I'd heard had the best selection of blues and jazz. It was the Dayton Record Store located at 824 Broadway on the corner of 12th street. We found many cool, out-of-print blues records on Chess, Checker and King Records for $1.99-$3.99. While searching through the bins, I picked up Muddy Waters, Sonny Boy Williamson, Howlin' Wolf, Freddie King, and Little Walter Records. Some of them had a hole punched on the top right corner. That didn't bother me; as a matter of fact, those records are still in my collection and have since gone up in value.

While I was shopping, a tall gentleman tapped me on the shoulder and asked if I'd like to have his guest tickets to the Watkins Glen Summer Jam Festival. His name, he said, was Mongo Santamaria.

"Wow! Thanks!" we replied.

He gave me and my friends three tickets, then said, "Have a good time, and if you're back in the city, come see us play at Kenny's Castaways on 84th Street."

He wrote his name and address on the back of my ticket, which I've kept all of these years. It's in my vault of rock treasures. We never made it to see him, but I did make it to The Watkins Glen Festival. The Allman Brothers, The Band, and The Grateful Dead were the only bands featured. All household names, and known back then as Super Groups. I will never, ever forget that festival. It was truly an amazing experience. My friends and I were far away from the stage, but of course we heard everything. It rained and it got muddy, similar to like what happened at Woodstock. After a while, believe it or not, I lost my friends that drove us up there. Thank God, I got lucky and hitched a ride back home with two crazy, fun girls I met and their friend who had a Volkswagen van.

Even though Duane Allman had passed away, all other original band members were playing. Guitarist Dickey Betts sure had a big order to fill. But, even without those dueling guitars, he managed to pull it off with the help of Greg Allman. Jerry Garcia and the Grateful Dead were Rockin' and The Band was at top form. They all played literally for hours upon hours, eventually to becoming a long jam session.

This festival was even larger than the crowd at Woodstock. As mentioned above, just three bands performed. An estimated 600,000 rock fans came to the Watkins Glen Grand Prix Raceway just outside Watkins Glen, New York, on July 28th, 1973. This was just three days after my birthday, and what a happy birthday it was! Glad my parents let me go. Without a doubt, this left a mark in Rock history.

Going back a couple of years, I did go to some memorable shows. The few I remember were at the Schaefer Music Festival, held in Central Park, New York.

In a beautiful outdoor setting, I had the rare pleasure of seeing Lee Michaels with Frosty, his drummer. They didn't play too much in the New York area. My God, they were incredibly loud, so much in fact, my ears were ringing for days. His organ was blasting, piercing through my ears. It was so cool when he played "Stormy Monday." That was my favorite tune on his debut album. Frosty was a solid, powerful drummer and, for being only two musicians, it was a great live show.

Terry Reid also played that day. His voice sounded like Steve Marriot to me. I'd never listened to him before so figured I'd purchase his debut album, which I enjoyed. Little did I know I'd be meeting him in person just decades later.

At Queens College Memorial Center, I got to see Mountain with Eric Mercury on November 14th 1969. Mountain was also incredibly loud! just as my ears were getting over the deafening sounds of Lee Michaels. Mountain was even louder! Never have I seen so many amplifiers on stage. It was my first time seeing them. I saw them again in 1970 at the Capitol Theater with Mylon and special guests. By far, the loudest band I've ever seen *to this day!* Guitarist Leslie West had six towering stacks of Sunn Amplifiers, and bassist Felix Pappalardi, just about the same. In those days, the unreal price of a concert ticket was $5.50 to see Mountain!

Also in 1970, I saw Delaney & Bonnie and Friends with Eric

Clapton and John Mayall, once again at Queens College Memorial Center. Dig this! I still have the original flyers with date listed and ticket stubs for these shows. Can you believe paying only $4.50 to see Delaney & Bonnie and John Mayall? You can't get a pack of gum nowadays at that price!

My trips to New York never felt long enough. Moving from New York City to the Midwest was quite a change. Culture shock at first, but I soon discovered a cool scene happening in music. I heard from a few friends that Chris Brubeck (jazz giant Dave Brubeck's son) was opening up a place where local musicians could drop by with their gear and have open jam sessions. At that time, Chris played in the band New Heavenly Blue. One of their band members, Peter "Madcat" Ruth, stopped by from time to time. What a Helluva blues harp player he was! Will never forget playing with Chris and Madcat plus many other musicians. What a fun time we had jamming. Chris Brubeck was a multi-talented musician. He played electric bass guitar, trombone, and piano. The place he secured was a very spacious studio where many musicians would have room to play together. It sure was loads of fun while it lasted. Around and about town, you could find fantastic outdoor concerts and clubs and bars to see new bands and old-school blues artists.

Commander Cody and his Lost Planet Airmen played lots of gigs in town. They were a fun band to see live. Seemed like a huge following in Ann Arbor for blues and blues rock, which was fine with me. As a matter of fact, my brother and I attended all three Ann Arbor Blues and Jazz Festivals in 1972, 1973 and 1974. All took place at The Otis Spann Memorial Field near Huron High School. They were five-day events of blues and jazz that I'll never forget.

As an avid collector of rock 'n' roll memorabilia and American pop culture, I still have the original ticket stubs and concert programs stored in one of my old, wooden wine cases for safe-keeping. I'm so happy that I had the opportunity to see some of my heroes of blues and jazz, such as Freddie King, Ray Charles, Muddy Waters, Howlin' Wolf, Jimmy Reed, Johnny Otis, Count

Basie and his Orchestra, Dr. John, Miles Davis, and Otis Rush, just to name a few. My dad let me borrow his 8mm camera to film some of the bands, but all I filmed was Muddy Waters; I was close to the stage but had no sound. It's in storage so maybe one day I'll have it copied and transferred onto DVD.

Looking back, on Friday December 10th, 1971, at the Crisler Arena (Now called the Crisler Center) located at the University of Michigan, my brother and I had tickets to The John Sinclair Freedom Rally Concert. This was in response to the imprisonment of John Sinclair, the political activist and jazz poet, for possession of marijuana. This event was much bigger than originally expected from the organizers of this concert. So much pot was flowing in the air at that massive event, you couldn't help getting a contact high from all the thick, lingering smoke. My head was spinning.

I vividly remember John Lennon walking onto the stage with Yoko Ono. David Peel introduced them. John picked up an acoustic guitar and played a few songs. Then, he picked up a National Steel Resonator Dobro guitar and played a song he wrote about John Sinclair. I remember the opening lyrics said, "It ain't fair, John Sinclair, let him be, set him free." Elephant's Memory was his backup band.

Stevie Wonder put on a great show, as did Bob Seger. I can't remember everything, but as the years passed, I learned that this event was filmed and released as *Ten for Two*, a documentary about John Sinclair. Personally, I've never seen the whole film; however, various videoclips you can view that have been loaded up on YouTube.

Sinclair also managed the MC5 and was very involved with music, as well as his political views. Shortly after the rally, he was granted freedom by the Michigan Supreme Court. Sinclair talked about John Lennon helping him out of his nine – ten-year sentence, knocking it down to two years. Stored in my files are the original concert pamphlet and a copy of the original contract from the Ann Arbor Federation of Musicians stating John Lennon and Yoko Ono to perform two songs with wages of $500.00 to be dispatched to the John Sinclair Freedom Fund at show's end. Through the years, my brother and I attended many memorable concerts in Ann Arbor and surrounding areas, as well as downtown Detroit. (As I was writing about these shows, I phoned my brother to see if he remembered some of them. He did, but not as many as I had. Glad my memory serves me well! LOL!

At Cobo Hall Arena on December 5th 1973, we had the rare experience of seeing Emerson, Lake and Palmer perform in *Quadraphonic Sound* for the very first time *Ever*! This auditorium was magnificent! Loudspeakers were situated all over the place. Greg Lake's vocals were unmistakable. We will never have anyone like him again in the music world. From his days playing with King Crimson to joining E.L.P, you'd get chills listening to his vocal range from soft to powerful, on several albums and live. Keith Emerson's keyboard madness was intense. That night, I heard the most insane moog synthesizer sounds wailing all around the auditorium. Can't forget about Carl Palmer either. One incredible drummer. For a three-piece band, they were outstanding. It's so sad to me that Carl is the only member left; Keith and Greg both passed away in 2016 unfortunately. Thankfully, they left us listeners plenty of recordings that will live on forever.

We also had the opportunity to see The Alice Cooper Band at Cobo Hall that same year on their Billion Dollar Babies Tour. It was another awesome show. The Michigan Palace was one of many cool places to see rock bands. We saw Slade, King Crimson, The Strawbs, and Hawkwind there.

Back then, there were many progressive rock bands playing, as well as your rock favorites. Not far from our home, at Gallup Park in Ann Arbor near Huron High School, Free summer concerts were held every Sunday. Usually, they featured local bands we'd already seen many times. Sometimes we went and sometimes we didn't.

But, after reading in the local newspaper that Johnny Winter was going to perform, my brother and I flew out of the house and drove out to see him. It was the last of the free summer shows, and we wouldn't have missed it for the world. We ran right up to the front of the stage and were excited (especially me) I admired Johnny Winter tremendously. He's one of my top three favorite guitarists of all time. It's beyond words how fast he played. Rick Derringer was fantastic also. Their dueling guitars were so much fun to watch, trading licks back and forth, fluid, smooth as silk and in sync!

After a couple of songs, Johnny picked up a bottle of Bali Hai wine and drank it on stage. I'll never forget, as it was a weird looking shaped bottle, something you'd see a captain and his crew drinking on a pirate ship. I found out years later that Bali Hai and Mateus Wine from Portugal were popular drinks in the late 1960s and early 1970s. Jimi Hendrix actually loved Mateus. I remember drinking it back then. Funny, I remember my girl-friend stuck a candle on top of the bottle when it was empty. because it looked cool and, I'll admit it did serve its purpose. Times have dramatically changed in the wine world. Can you imagine a current rock star guzzling port wine?

It was a great, live, fun show that I'll never forget.

♪ ♩ ♪

Sadly, things changed for our family on November 5th 1972. It happened on a Sunday. My father and I would usually play racquetball on the weekends at the University of Michigan, and we played a few games that Sunday. Then a couple of college students challenged us. My father was a damn good player and, to be honest, so was I. We accepted and played a couple of games. After winning both, we shook hands with our opponents and left.

While driving back home, I noticed my father was breathing a little heavy, but he said he was okay and "Just settling down from playing."

When we arrived home, things seemed normal. I took a shower, got dressed then went back in my bedroom and made a phone call to one of my friends on campus at University of Michigan, then told my parents I'd be back later. Upon leaving,

I noticed the bathroom door was open with my father sitting on the toilet seat with his clothes on and his hands on his head facing down. I thought it looked quite strange, didn't think too much about it and left.

Later, when I got back, there were paramedics present carrying out my father on a stretcher. His eyes were closed, but I couldn't tell if he was dead or alive. He was rushed immediately to the University of Michigan Hospital.

Our family was extremely worried. We waited in the hospital guest room, praying solemnly. At 10:00 pm, he was pronounced dead.

"We did everything we could to save him," the surgeon said "The blood flow was blocked from a buildup of plaque inside the artery walls." Officially: atherosclerosis of coronary arteries. In short, a heart attack.

Dad was only fifty-one years old at the time.

From that day on, life would never be the same, especially for my mother. I had a really hard time, thinking it was my fault for playing the four games of racquetball that killed him.

At that time, hospitals were in the developmental stage of pacemakers, and although technology was advancing, they were just not prepared and set up to save my father's life. To this day, I still can't understand why and how this happened at such an early age? Dad had been a chiropractor prior to being a salesman and always exercised. He played many sports, swam laps in the pool, and played golf. It just didn't make any sense to me at all.

He did achieve everything he always wanted and planned for before his passing, a family he loved, a comfortable house & a well-paying job. I remember how happy he was when he purchased our house. We were happy too, after living in an apartment building for so many years. Now we had the freedom of no one living above or below us, no one on either side.

I'm so glad that he lived in our home for at least one year before leaving this earth. Since then, I've had many dreams of going back in time, trying to change what happened and saving his life.

My mother was working, but it was tough supporting three children. So, my brother and I looked for jobs in town. I worked briefly at a record store part time and still played music on a regular basis. I was close to eighteen years old at that time. Just barely done with high school.

Still, my brother and I continued going to many concerts. From the years 1972 -1974, we went to see Delaney & Bonnie and Friends at Hill Auditorium at the University of Michigan. This time Billy Preston was playing keyboards with them, and another artist Iris Bell, a jazz vocalist and pianist whom I had never heard of before, was on the bill.

At the Bowen Fieldhouse in Ypsilanti, which was the next town over, we caught Chuck Berry with The Drifters, Teegarden & Van Winkle, and The Woolies. That was an unusual show. The Woolies were from Lansing, Michigan, and had a hit "Who Do You Love." Teegarden and Van Winkle were a duo Band from Tulsa, Oklahoma. We'd never heard of these two bands, but I do remember they were pretty good. We just wanted to see Chuck Berry!

We saw Stevie Wonder with The Ike and Tina Turner Revue at the Crisler Arena in 1971. Still have the ticket stub. Now that was an electrifying Show! In 1974, at The Read Fieldhouse in Kalamazoo, Humble Pie played with Spooky Tooth and Montrose. Wow! that was an exciting time to see these bands. Steve Marriot was spitting at people in the front rows which was disgusting. Don't remember why . . . but it was entertaining to me.

Humble Pie put on a great show. Spooky Tooth was awesome too. Loved both of these British bands and had all their records up to that point, including Montrose. As for Montrose, they were rocking. This was when Sammy Hagar was their vocalist, way before joining Van Halen. Living in Michigan for a few years, I was finally getting used to life in the Midwest. A great rock 'n' roll scene was happening at that time. I'd made quite a few friends and so had my brother and sister.

In 1973, I received a letter from Walt Disney Productions recommending training for me in a good fundamental art school to support my talent in drawing cartoons. I excelled in art from grade school through high school going back to the drawings I'd do on my grandmother's music sheets as a kid. My mother encouraged me, stating I could combine my music with art and told me, "Your father always said you would be headed towards working in a studio."

Deep down, I knew she was right. I often wondered what would have happened, but decided my path was music.

I decided to attend a Summer Institute at Berklee College of Music in Boston, Massachusetts, wanting to further my studies in music. I studied music theory, arranging, melody, improvisation and transposition. While residing in the dorms, I got together with a few student musicians and formed a blues band to play on the weekends at local clubs in town.

One gig we played was located in the Combat Zone. I had no idea what I was getting myself into. In the 1960's, many strip clubs, peep shows, X-rated movie theatres, adult bookstores and a wide array of crime and prostitution took place right there.

The club we played at had a predominately black audience. We weren't afraid or anything, just brought our equipment in and played our normal setlist. Our combo sounded exceptionally tight that night. People cheered!

After our set was over, we took a break. While drinking a beer, this large woman came up to our table and said to me, "Honey, you sound just like B.B. King." When I got up to shake her hand, she hugged me. I thought all my bones would crack! She was huge! I'll never forget what she said to me though. It made me feel very good especially being just a skinny white boy. When we were packing up our gear, one of the bartenders came up to our band and said, "You guys, this is a bad neighborhood. Shady characters, pickpockets, you name it! Be careful out here. I'll call you a cab."

Well, I loved jazz, but I just wasn't ready to learn such sophisticated improvisational charts. And in all honestly, Berklee School of Music was for very serious and focused musicians. Furthermore, I just loved rock 'n' roll too much. Well, it was an interesting experience for me, and I did learn a lot in that short time.

When I came back home that summer, I decided to have a big party. I invited all my friends over. Many were musicians, a few professional artists plus my schoolmates. They drove in from Detroit, Ann Arbor, and neighboring towns. Two girls that came from Detroit with a few friends of mine were the Thom sisters, Nancy and Judy. Their Father owned the Harmony House record store chain. I was blown away. It was headquartered in Hazel Park, a Detroit suburb. At one point they had around thirty-eight stores!

Well, getting back to my party, it was loud and crazy. Lots of drinking. A towering two-piece wooden cabinet fell down, partly on Judy Thom! All these books came flying down on her and hit a few other people on the head as well. Everyone freaked out.

I asked Judy, "Are you okay?" She just laughed at me. Thank God, she wasn't hurt. I was thinking, I could have been sued.

People were there whom I'd never met; they were friends of friends. One interesting character was a hard-core rocker who told me he was assembling a powerhouse band a la New York Dolls meets MC5 meets Iggy Pop and The Stooges. He was a bit older than me, but we were on the same page when it came to music we enjoyed. When he told me his name, I thought, *What the fuck? Sirius Trixon?*

"What kind of whacky name is that?" I asked.

"I was named after the brightest star visible from earth. The constellation Canis Major the Greater Dog. AKA the Dog Star," he said.

I thought he was high on drugs. But he said, "I don't do drugs. It's for real."

Anyway, he told me to keep in touch, which I did. Quite a party, that one. Stains were all over our carpet. My mother was pissed! We had it cleaned by the following week.

♪♫♪

In 1974, I was nineteen and I frequented many shows in town at bars, clubs and the like. Lots of blues' bands played at a place called the Blind Pig. I hung out there, drinking beer and listening to John Lee Hooker, Koko Taylor and Roosevelt Sykes. Many local artists played in town a lot, like SRC and The Rationals.

In 1972, Michigan had reduced its drinking age from twenty-one to eighteen. It became one of the first states experimenting with lowering the drinking age. However, following a rise in drunk-driving accidents, Michigan also became the first state to move it's drinking age back to twenty-one in 1978.

When in town shopping, I used to hear Jim McCarty playing guitar, just practicing at the John Sinclair House on Hill Street. He must have been living there, I thought, as a window was wide open, and that's where the music was coming from. Just standing there listening to his fantastic licks, I'd be in awe. Jim originally played with Mitch Ryder and the Detroit Wheels in the 1960's and he performed with other bands such as Cactus, Detroit and The Rockets. Cactus rocked the house! They were great to see live. To me, Ann Arbor was like a hippie-blues-rock kind of town with a cool funky vibe.

A few friends came over to jam downstairs in our family home's basement (guess you could call it our playroom). They left their equipment overnight. We jammed on the weekends. Bass, drums and me on guitar. Decades later, my sister told me that when we weren't around, she and her girlfriends would play our instruments. When I heard that, I just had to laugh.

More changes were about to hit my family. My mother had been studying to be a gerontologist. She attended the University of Michigan to get her degree. When she graduated, she had an opportunity to teach in Southern California. She decided to move our family there.

So, with that said, we close the Summer of 1974.

♪♫♪

Mom sold the home we had all loved in Ann Arbor and rented one with a pool in Woodland Hills, in the San Fernando Valley. She taught at USC for several years in the late 1970's and at one point was even featured in the "View" section of the *Los Angeles*

Times. I was incredibly proud of her, but never told her until she worked at the Marriott Hotel in Newport Beach years later. She told me that was her favorite job she ever had and her favorite place to live.

So, there I was, for the first time, living in Southern California, diggin' the scene unlike anywhere I have ever lived before. Within the first week of September 1974, I received a letter from that Sirius Trixon, the dude I mentioned earlier, explaining that he had the backing for forming a band with me and fellows named Billy, Spencer and Rick. Funding was coming from a very wealthy family that owned Lafayette Towers in downtown Detroit, which were two massive apartment buildings with breathtaking views. They had agreed to back us up with amplifiers, guitars, and all necessary equipment to get the band off the ground. I believe $20,000 was the magic number provided. Donnie Bishop from Showtime Productions, who also managed Brownsville Station, was appointed our manager. Brownsville Station had a huge hit back then, "Smokin' in the Boys Room," which was later covered by Motley Crue in 1985.

Motor City Bad Boys was the name of the band chosen by lead vocalist Sirius Trixon beforehand. T-shirts and bumper stickers were already designed and being produced, and we hadn't even met, practiced, or recorded one note yet. To me that was quite strange and surprising. Little did I know that Trixon would spring more strange surprises in the months to come, some of them with devastating effects.

Well, as the story goes, I took a plane trip back to Michigan, which was paid for in advance by management. The two brothers who financed this venture also owned a travel agency called Gulliver's Travel, Inc. I took my Gibson SG with me, packed my luggage full of clothes, and told my mother I'd be back, but I didn't want to miss this opportunity.

Upon arrival, I met the chosen band members for the Motor City Bad Boys. Billy Wimble, Guitar; Spencer "Spence" Hirsch, Drums; and Rick Lockhart, Bass. Trixon couldn't sing too well to say the least, but his stage performance, well, that was a of a different story.

We first rehearsed in an old, musical-instrument store called Massimino Music. It was at their old location before moving to their new place on 13 Mile Road. Then they moved us to a new location in downtown Detroit. We rented that place for only $200 a month, and moved our equipment to a studio that was shared with the band The Romantics. They were starting out just like us, but from 1977 on, those guys had many hit songs such as "What I Like About You," and "Talking in Your Sleep "and had their Greatest commercial success in the mid 1980's.

The equipment we chose was Marshall Amplification. Two full stacks for each guitarist. Gotta say, before all this happened, I could only dream of owning Marshall amplifiers. This was the first band I ever played in that got any recognition. Billy played a Gibson Gold Top with two white, P-90 soap pickups and a Dan Armstrong clear, Lucite guitar made by Ampeg (like Keith Richards played with the Rolling Stones).

I played a Gibson Les Paul Junior with two black, dog ear P-90'pickups. It was a 1955 Dark Sunburst Les Paul which had been modified with an extra pickup and had four gold-tone, volume-control knobs. It played like a dream. At that time, I sold my 1970 Gibson SG at a profit. I had an old, faded, Pink Fender Stratocaster. But as much as I liked playing it, the Les Paul just had this real dirty, ballsy, rich tone that I loved. The sustain and controlled feedback I was able to achieve was insane! Interestingly, from that point on, I played only Les Paul guitars.

As a band we wrote a whole bunch of songs but only recorded four. Three of them were written by Trixon and me. Trixon had these extreme delusions. He often referred to us as your Jagger/ Richards team of songwriters. Yeah, he was some character. He had a scraggly rooster haircut and wanted to be known as The Legendary Sirius Trixon, The Best Punk Rock Vocalist That Ever Lived! The rest of the fellas in our band, including me, often wondered what he was thinking. We thought he acted more like a poser/male groupie than an actual vocalist in a rock band. He always wanted to go backstage. He did many other odd things that we thought were nuts.

Well, it was time to record, and we were ready, set to go after practicing for many months. The four original songs that we recorded were done in one take with no overdubs at United Sound Studios. This was around December of 1974, but I don't recall what day to be exact. The studio was situated at the corner of Second Avenue and Antoinette in Midtown, Detroit, and has had an unbelievable history. Better known today as United Sound Systems, it was founded in 1933 and was Detroit's first major recording studio!

The songs that we recorded were as follows: "Bad Boys Gang," "Hollywood Queen," "Out in the Streets" and "Big Time Bum." Even though each band member was handed a copy of the original tapes, to this day, those songs have never seen the light of day. Who knows? Maybe one day I could get clearance. If not, they may never be released.

The audio engineers at the soundboard that were recording us said we were the second white-only group besides the MC5 that ever recorded there. But they commented on diggin' our sound and were impressed that we played all songs through, live, with no breaks in between. Just straight, pure rock!

To give you an idea of other bands, groups, and vocalists that recorded there through the years, here ya go: Aretha Franklin, Albert King, Parliament Funkadelic, The Dramatics, Isaac Hayes, Gladys Knight and The Pips, John Lee Hooker and Jackie Wilson.

Our managers sent Motor City Bad Boys tapes out to almost every record label. One letter that arrived at our office particularly surprised me. It was from Steve Paul, at that time the owner of Blue-Sky Records. Previously, he had been the owner of The Scene Club in New York. That place shaped the music of the 1960's and inspired jam sessions from just about every top band and musician you could think of. He also managed Johnny Winter. Steve Paul wrote that he loved the tapes! A few others wrote notes as well. Rick Derringer, who played with Johnny, wrote a note about both Billy and me, stating we sounded awesome. He said he loved the lead guitar work—*My lead guitar work!* Loved

Johnny and Rick, so you know how much that meant to me personally. Damn, just wish I had that letter for keepsake! Guess it's still in the hands of our management company. Mercury, MCA and Arista Records were also interested in us.

We visited the Mercury Records office first to see what might transpire. We were told by our manager after their meeting that the label wanted us to record more demos with more songs. That was their request and that's about all I can recall. Not much else occurred afterwards.

Reflecting on those years 1974–1975, Rick, our bass player, just happened to have a job at The Michigan Palace working lights and other duties. Our band got to see KISS Live plenty of times, as well as The New York Dolls when they were out promoting their *Too Much Too Soon* album. Almost every time they played in Detroit; we were there.

One weekend, we drove out to see KISS in Flint, Michigan, which was a way's drive, but we had a good time. We followed both bands. Arthur, Jerry and Syl from The Dolls were approachable and pretty laidback. Johnny and David always went their separate ways.

The Dolls hired this guy, Frenchy, who was their valet. It seemed to me that he did a lot more, as he acted like their tour or road manager and would always help them out in many situations, difficult or not. He always dressed hip and usually blew a whistle to signal the start of a typical Dolls show. He used that whistle for other things as well. Pretty fun guy; nutty but cool.

We got to be friends with Junior and Moose, the roadies from KISS. They were big dudes and so long as you didn't fuck with them, you'd be okay. Ace was friendly and the only member of KISS that didn't have a huge ego. Paul, Peter and Gene, after their gigs, split off to be with their girlfriends. We had backstage passes for just about every time they played in town.

One funny story about KISS was after one of their gigs, they went back to their hotel. My band was hanging out in the lobby waiting to find out where the party we heard they were having would be. Anyway, this good-looking girl thought I was Paul.

This took place around 1974, and my hair was basically the same as his; long, black and curly. I'm from New York, so this girl couldn't tell the difference. I just played along and guess you can figure out the rest of this story.

Here's a little trivia: The Motor City Bad Boys purchased our platform boots at the same place KISS purchased theirs. But their boots were custom-made, with intricate work done. Ours were just solid colors. It was a shop on Yonge Street in Toronto, Canada.

At the Michigan Palace, we also got in to see UFO, Rush, Blue Oyster Cult, Ted Nugent, and Bob Seger and The Silver Bullet Band. Bob Seger played a lot in Michigan. I got to be friends with Charlie Martin, their drummer. On a sad note, I found out years later that on his way home from a band rehearsal, Charlie got hit by a motorist and the injury left him unable to walk again. This happened in February of 1977.

The Michigan Palace was an outstanding auditorium to see bands perform. We had the opportunity to practice there one night during the week. Rick was able to have us setup and play for a couple of hours. What a feeling it was, having the whole auditorium to ourselves! It felt great. Our first time on a big stage playing as loud as we wanted. Of course, no audience was there except for our girlfriends and sound crew, plus two of our roadies. Funny thing: Aerosmith was practicing there just before we arrived.

One afternoon I swung by to see Rick. To my surprise, Capt. Beefheart was on the stage for a soundcheck. He was yelling and screaming at his soundman, "I can't hear myself! Turn up the fucking volume!" Then he yelled again, "Dammit! Shit! Fuck!"

It was hilarious. He was like spastic, jumping up and down, swaying, swearing and carrying on.

Another crazy episode was when Ted Nugent was running after some punk thief who swiped his notorious Gibson Birdland guitar right out of his dressing room! Ted grabbed a heavy link chain and flew after this little fucker. In the end, he got his guitar back. Wow, I'll never forget that scene!

Rick was the only guy in our band who was working at that

time. As far as where I lived, it was at Jim Jam's mother's house. (That was his nickname; his real name is James Messner.) On the night shift he worked at a bakery. We used to tease him, saying, "Hey, Jim Jam, make a lotta dough today?" He was our road manager/spiritual advisor. This home was not in the best neighborhood. One day, when our guitarist, Billy, stepped out of the front porch doorway, he got randomly shot at by some gang-bangers driving up the street. He was lucky that the bullet was found under his lung and the operation was a success. Holy Shit, that was one scary moment!

Trixon lived there too. It was a big house in Highland Park, Metro Detroit, with two floors and a big basement. We had our own limo driver named Robbie who would pick us up from time to time. My God, I was starting to feel like a rock star, but knew there was lots of work to be done up this road to fame.

One weekend we were invited to be interviewed by Ronnie Legg, a well-known disc jockey on CJOM FM Radio, Windsor, Ontario, Canada. This radio station was located right over the border from Detroit. What a blast we had! I still couldn't believe all this stuff was happening without playing any clubs or concert halls. We just went along in hopes of making it.

We took nothing for granted. We practiced a lot and we sounded tight. Six months had passed since the band had formed and we were just about ready to perform live. But the members of the band, including me, had our doubts about our vocalist; wondered where he was going and how to deal with his vocal challenges. We often wondered, how could this band make it in less than one year?

At this time, Grand Funk Railroad was the most recognized rock band in Michigan. They had a huge place in Flint, which was about seventy miles away from Detroit. Our manager took us out to visit them one day. I vaguely remember meeting them, but will never forget how much land they owned and the beautiful scenery high up in the mountains.

Not long after, our band planned a trip to New York. We wanted to check out the music scene there and possibly line up some future gigs. One of the first places we visited was Club CBGB. We spoke with Hilly, the owner, about performing there someday. He showed us around. There was a band playing when we walked in, and they sounded pretty awful. It was a sound-check, I supposed.

I asked who was playing. "The Cramps," Hilly said. "Do you know them?"

"I do, but I haven't listened to much of their stuff."

Little did I know what a huge cult following they had. Even today, they have a tremendous number of fans.

The next place we visited was the 82 Club. What an eccentric, bizarre place that was. It had been a famous drag club in the 1950's and 1960's

The 82 Club opened in 1953 and was operated by the Mafia, as most gay clubs were during that time. This club built a reputation as a desired hangout for celebrities who wanted to walk on the wild side—and it was wild, all right! Crazy place to be or be seen. Two rough and tough lesbians, Tommy, who worked the door, and Butchie, who ran the bar, managed the place. I wouldn't mess with either one of them, that's for sure. They kept everyone in line; but on occasion, when anyone caused trouble, look out!

Upon entering, we noticed these large-sized posters of some of the famous Drag Queens that had performed there in the past hanging up in the lobby. Around 1972 or so, they started turning Wednesday nights over to bands on the glitter rock scene. When Max's Kansas City closed their doors for the first time in late 1974, Club 82 became the place to party. It finally faded out in late 1975–1976, and by that time Max's had re-opened. But during that 1972–1973 period, David Bowie, Blondie, New York Dolls, Wayne County, The Ramones, John Waters & Divine, Lou Reed, and even the Rolling Stones frequented there. We figured if the Dolls played at this club, it would be cool for us to give it a go. But our amplifiers and Spencer's drum kit would never fit on such a small stage. We just shook our heads and left.

Moving on, we hung out in the East Village for a while.

Visited Katz Delicatessen and ordered corned beef and pastrami sandwiches. They were huge! All sandwiches were filled with extra sauerkraut, spicy mustard, and French dressing with a kosher pickle. They were *So* good. Our tummies were full the whole day. That was then, as for now I'm not vegan, but I quit eating red meat many years ago.

From there we walked over to Gem Spa, ordered a chocolate egg cream and picked up a *Rock Scene* magazine and other related music trades. Then we visited many local record stores: Bleeker Bob's, House of Oldies, Venus Records, Norman's Sound and Vision. After that, I brought the boys over to Wo Hop's Chinese Restaurant at 17 Mott Street in Chinatown for dinner. Walking down a flight of stairs that went on forever, the guys wondered, Where the hell is this restaurant?

But, when we were seated and the food came, everyone was happy. Man, those butterfly shrimps were just as delicious as the first time I ever tasted years ago. Roasted Duck Lo Mein, Wo Hop Chow Mai Fon, and Wor Won Ton Soup. Simply the best! It's amazing to me that after seventy years, this place still rocks. To top it off, it's open seven days a week, from 10:30 a.m. to 9: 00 p.m. However, back in the day, they used to be open til 4:30 in the morning. For decades, after clubbing all night, many celebrities, rock bands, and city workers have gone to this iconic restaurant.

The next day we visited shops like Granny Takes a Trip, located on the upper east end, and Jumping Jack Flash, checking out all the hip, trendy clothing and hi-heeled platform shoes and boots. Trash and Vaudeville was another cool place. We purchased a few things such as shoes, boots, and custom wide-striped tee shirts for all the band members in electric blue, fire engine red and hot pink. Those clothes were unfortunately stolen by one of our roadies who was a fucking thief and, to top it off, had a drug habit as well. So, yeah, we fired him. A few groupies also stole some of our stuff. Yes, we had a few that followed us around.

At the end of our trip to New York, we went to see a few bands playing in town. Richard Hell, Blondie, The Ramones and The New York Dolls. When we flew back to Detroit, all sorts of crazy stuff happened.

Upon arrival, believe it or not—and I don't remember how it even happened—KISS set up this contest on Radio WWW 106 FM in Detroit, for me to win this Gibson Midnight Special L6 Guitar! I still have the waiver I had to sign, dated January 8th 1975. Honestly, think I gave it away to Blackie when I joined the Killer Kane Band just a few months later. It was ugly-looking to me and I didn't like the way it played. It was the same color (black) that Paul Stanley of KISS played a lot.

Finally, the day we were waiting for. On May 21st 1975, at the Latin Quarters on 3067 E. Grand Blvd. in Detroit, The Motor City Bad Boys played their Premier Gala Performance. Tickets were only $6.00 at the door and $5.00 in advance. Unbelievable in today's world! We were written up in the *Detroit Free Press* with a mixed review and were compared to KISS, Iggy Pop and the Stooges, and Alice Cooper. A small segment in *CREEM* magazine also mentioned us.

Spencer's drum kit was placed inside a genuine 1957 Pink Cadillac. It was the front half of the body and was custom made by his father. It also included actual working headlights that were rigged and turned on with a flick of the switch. This prop was set up on a wooden platform so Spencer could see every band member while playing. When he turned on the switch while we were setting up, it blew out a fuse before our show even started! Billy was at right front of the stage facing the audience, and I was to the left near Rick, our bass player. As for Sirius, he was running around all over the place swinging his microphone . . . almost smacking a girl's head in the front row from the stage. He loved Iggy, so he imitated his antics on stage, but the effect wasn't remotely close. He yelled and warned audience, "No dancing allowed!" And he did everything in his power to not let that happen.

Our band was seriously loud that evening. The place was packed! This theater we played at had hosted some of the biggest music acts of that time; Stevie Wonder, Etta James, James Brown, The Temptations, Ray Charles, Al Green, Sammy Davis, Jr., and The Four Tops had all played there at various times in the '60's and part of the '70's. In the 1980's, bands like the Red-Hot Chili Peppers, Nick Cave and the Bad Seeds, Sonic Youth, Jane's Addiction, Nine Inch Nails, and The Cramps played there, right up until plans to demolish the theatre were announced in 2008.

The building sat vacant until late December of 2011 when it was finally torn down for good. End of an era. We played for a little over an hour that night with no encore. Just straight, solid rock 'n' roll. Billy and I traded dueling guitar licks and, I have to say, we sounded really good. Spencer and Rick kept that low, bottom beat going smoothly throughout our show. We had a party backstage afterwards with food and drinks.

Can you imagine, with all this going on and what we prepared for and practiced for, *it all went straight to Hell!*

Yep, just a few weeks later, when we were offered to tour with Humble Pie, our band broke up.

The breakup was due to the major collisions we had with our lead singer, "The Legendary Sirius Trixon The Best Punk Rock Vocalist That Ever Lived!" about who controlled publishing, how much we were paid, and so forth. It was a huge mess of conflict, confusion and disillusionment. In the end, with pure disgust, management offered each band member a one-way ticket back to wherever they chose. I flew back to sunny California to be with my family, and I never looked back. The rest of the band was from Detroit, so I'm sure management was happy about eliminating that extra expense.

I couldn't fucking believe what had just happened. All I could think about was, at least I had my 1955 Les Paul Junior to bring back home with me, as well as my rock-star wardrobe. Turned out, Sirius continued to keep the band alive by putting together a new bunch of musicians under the Sirius Trixon and The Motor City Bad Boys banner. They toiled in semi-obscurity until 1980, then disbanded forever.

So, I returned to California. After settling in at my mother's place, I received a phone call from Arthur Kane, the bass player from the New York Dolls. I was stunned. I had to ask him how he got my phone number . . . I figured it was from James Sliman, The Dead Boys' road manager, with whom I was good friends. James was one of the few people I'd met out on the road that I gave my number to. It made sense as the Dead Boys, Dictators, New York Dolls, and The Ramones all knew each member of the Motor City Bad Boys.

James had written several letters and postcards to me while on tour with the Dead Boys after they signed with Sire Records. We kept in touch through the years. He was a photographer as well as tour manager, and took several photos of the Killer Kane Band.

So, this phone call came around late June 1975. I was just hanging out by the pool at my mother's home. Arthur told me he was assembling a new band, then mentioned this guy named Blackie who played guitar, was a vocalist, and had written a few songs. They both wanted me to meet up with them in Hollywood. Arthur told me he liked my guitar playing, saying I reminded him of Johnny Thunders with those same raunchy, trashy, slashing killer tones from my guitar and amplifier.

At that time, while on tour in Florida, drummer Jerry Nolan and guitarist Johnny Thunders abruptly left the Dolls and went back to New York. Both were struggling with drug and alcohol addiction, and friction within the band was extremely high. As the story goes, one night, when staying at a Trailer Park/Motel owned by Jerry's mother, Nolan and Thunders announced that they were leaving the band. That surely seemed like the end of the New York Dolls. Sylvain Sylvain and Malcolm McLaren headed off to New Orleans. As for David Johansen and the band's roadies, I have no idea where they finally ended up. Poor Arthur was stranded, but thanks to Blackie, who replaced Thunders for only a couple of gigs, he made plans to form a new band in Hollywood.

Blackie's real name is Steven Edward Duren, but he went by the stage name Blackie Goozeman. Years later, when he formed the heavy-metal band W.A.S.P., he changed his stage name again to Blackie Lawless, as it remains today. So, at this point, Arthur, David and Syl had one last chance to sort things out, but they knew it would never be the same, and it never panned out.

Blackie, who was one of Arthur's old friends from the Bronx, decided to head on out to Los Angeles. That's where The Killer Kane Band was formed. We met up in a studio at the drummer's house, located on Lookout Mountain in Laurel Canyon. His name was Michael O'Brian. Michael lived high up in the mountains with his wife and daughter.

One afternoon, we both visited Jan Berry, from Jan and Dean fame. Michael was friends with him as they were neighbors. I was well-aware of Jan's terrible car accident in 1966 when he smashed his Corvette and was left paralyzed with severe brain damage. You could call that accident "Dead Man's Curve" which, ironically, was a hit song written for them in 1964 by Brian Wilson. Jan was left with a speech impediment, but our visit was quite pleasant. I shook his hand when leaving. Sadly, he passed away in March of 2004 at sixty-two from a brain seizure.

Many celebrities lived in this area. Laurel Canyon has so much deep history. Frank Zappa's home was located just below that hill. The late great master magician, Harry Houdini, resided right down that same hill, but that was in 1919, more than a hundred years ago. Singer/songwriter blues-harp player John Mayall also lived high up on Lookout Mountain.

We practiced for a while at Michael's home. Later on, we shared a studio in Los Angeles with a power-pop band, The Quick. Danny Benair, their drummer, was a nice guy, and Steven, their guitarist, played some tasty guitar licks. I heard them practicing one day when arriving early. Really cool, melodic pop band; they kind of reminded me of the band Sparks.

While all this was happening, I was seeking work and ran across M.S. Distributing's ad for a Music Distributor. Their new West Coast warehouse was hiring many positions in Sun Valley. Chicago is where their main offices and other warehouse were located.

When I got hired, I initially pulled orders, then worked in shipping and receiving, as well as the returns department. After a few months I advanced to working in an office with the buyers.

My last promotion at M.S. Distributing was working out in the field servicing record merchandisers like City One Stop, Licorice Pizza, Music Plus, Peaches, and select Tower Records stores. My job lasted from 1975–1977.

One story I must mention, which still haunts me to this day, is about one of my dear friends, Shelly Ann Bolo. Her sister, Wendy Bolo, introduced me to her. Wendy and I both worked together at M.S. Dist. Shelly was working for Polygram Distribution at the time and had been with them for several years. We used to run into each other on the road and traded Promo LPs when we met. She gave me a lot of great stuff! We became good friends. She always had a smile on her face and was fun to hang out with. She was a free-spirited beautiful gal.

Sadly, in the Lifelines section of *Billboard* magazine, September 23rd, 1978, issue, they announced Shelly's death. She was only twenty-four years old. Truth be told, she was at the wrong place at the wrong time and got stabbed to death near Griffin Park in Los Angeles. Police believed it was the work of the Hillside Strangler, a serial killer who was terrorizing Los Angeles. But L.A.P.D. either never knew or never revealed the truth, as there were copycat murders at that horrible time in Los Angeles. This story was also told in the *Los Angeles Times* newspaper. I often think about her. Wendy was devastated. We got to be closer from that time on. Wendy was the one who informed me of her sister's passing and its horrible circumstances.

Getting back to M.S. Dist., the one thing that I'll never forget was the promotion for the band Blondie. We distributed the Private Stock label, which was a small independent that shut down in 1978. Other notable artists on that label at the time were Robert Gordon, Frankie Valli, Michael Zager Band, and Starbuck. I remember shipping out a whole load of Blondie posters featuring Deborah Harry wearing a see-through blouse. Every freaking store in the world wanted that poster badly. On the bottom of the poster, it read "Blondie on Private Stock Records and GRT Tapes." That very poster has been featured up for sale at many rock auction houses. Who knew it would be a valuable collector's item someday? Wish I'd kept a few, but at least I still have the original vinyl pressing and a Blondie Valentine's Day card with a black-and-white 8x10 promotional photo. Guess that's better than nothing.

M.S Distributing shut down towards the end of 1977, and in that same location around 1978, another music company, Pickwick International, opened their doors. I worked there for just one year. Thinking back on it, I was the only person in our band with a regular daytime job except for Jimi Image, our second designated drummer. That was his stage name; Jimi Moore was his real name. I don't know where Blackie found him, but he was truly a solid drummer. He was also a pretty strange fellow. Funny, too. I visited him one day and he was eating raw hamburger meat!

"What the Hell, Jimi!" I yelled. "Are you nuts?"

He just smiled and said, "It has good protein."

OMG! Anyway, Michael just got fed up with all sorts of shit that piled up on him and left the band frustrated. While playing with Killer Kane, we visited and hung out at many a club scene: Whiskey A Go Go, The Rainbow, The Starwood, The Troubadour, The Roxy Theatre, The Palace and The L.A. Forum. Hell, the list goes on and on.

I had a few girlfriends while living in Southern California, and those few were a lot to handle. One girlfriend (who'll remain nameless) phoned my drummer up one evening asking for me and said if I wasn't there, she would slit her wrists! He called me that same night yelling at me to "Get this bitch help, *Now!*" Then he asked me, how in the hell did she even get my phone number in the first place? She was a wild one. I guess when you play with a rock band, these things can happen—if not too often.

Regardless, I did have fun with her, and she knew all of the hip, happening parties from the San Fernando Valley to Hollywood. The stories of parties and clubbing, I'll be writing about throughout this book but in no specific order. They really need to be talked about, especially for a guy like me who just stepped right into this crazy world of music celebrity status.

One party we attended was at the home of Danny Hutton (vocalist from Three Dog Night). It was his birthday. He lived in North Hollywood at the time. Right when I arrived with my crazy girlfriend, I heard a whole bunch of people singing in the kitchen. They sounded great.

"Who's that guy in the middle, wearing suspenders?" I asked a woman standing nearby.

"That's Lowell George from Little Feet. Don't you recognize him?" she asked.

I was afraid to say no, so I said, "Oh, yeah." I don't think she believed me.

Anyway, David Crosby, Graham Nash, Spencer Davis, Harry Nilsson, Chuck Negron, and members of The Electric Light Orchestra, I immediately recognized. I could not believe that all these musicians and songwriters were all in this house at the same time. I don't think I was starstruck, but I'll tell you, I was completely astonished. It's not every day you'd see this type of gathering. Hors d'oeuvres and cold beer were served. In another room, I was just goofing off playing electric piano, when Hugh McDowell from E.L O. came over to join me. He was their cello player; guess he also played other instruments I was not aware of.

We had lots of fun at that party. A night to remember, for sure.

Another party we went to was also in the mid-1970's.

Honestly, I don't remember who told us about this party, but we went. It was at drummer Buddy Miles' pad. I think he was renting this place out in Hollywood at the time. Wow! Every music celebrity you could think of was there! The place was packed with people! My girlfriend and I got terribly drunk. When walking into the bathroom to take a pee, I noticed a gold toilet seat. The whole toilet was in sparkling GOLD! To this day I still remember how strange that was.

Well, finally we met Buddy Miles. He was smiling, greeting everyone and having a great time. Me and my girlfriend had a fun time as well. What a crazy cool party.

Here's something you may not know about Buddy. In 1978, he was arrested and jailed for grand theft auto and for stealing from a clothing store in Hollywood. He served seven years in prison; first at the California Institution for Men at Chino, and then at San Quentin State Prison. He formed bands in both institutions, performing for groups of inmates. Here's a quote from *The Dallas Observer* in 1997: "When I went to prison, nobody put me in prison but Buddy Miles, okay? I paid for it; I served my time." Sadly, that was a tough time for him. However, Buddy continued playing till his passing in 2008 at age 60. His music will live on, though, from his days playing with The Electric Flag and Jimi Hendrix in the Band of Gypsys.

On most any given weekend at The Rainbow Bar and Grill in Hollywood, you'd find a whole bunch of familiar faces. One night, Blackie and I went upstairs to the Rainbow Room, which was a private part of the Rainbow for VIPs to chill out in a somewhat relaxed environment. We were having drinks, talking to a few girls and after a while (probably from drinking earlier), he was stone drunk and, out of nowhere, decided to urinate right out in the open! Everyone in that room was as stunned as I was! From that moment, I knew trouble was coming. Two bouncers spotted this happening and threw him out on his ass on the sidewalk—just like a movie. It was nuts! Thank God, I was escorted out. From what I remember, I drove him back to where he was staying at the time.

On other occasions, things were a bit more subdued, but they eventually got out of hand. Yep, that was my rock 'n' roll world back then. Crazy times. Our band sometimes had dinner at the Rainbow and could be drinking beer or having a cocktail. Pizza was the only thing on the menu I'd eat there. It was close to New York-style and tasty. Many notable rockers would come by to say hello at our table. Blackie was friends with Ace Frehley from KISS, for example. I can still hear Tony saying, "Will the movie stars please keep on moving. We have to clear this aisle!"

Tony was basically the floor manager at the Rainbow. Back then, on the weekends, that place was always busy and, at times, totally out of control. Whenever I had to go to the bathroom, I'd encounter this long line. Funny thing is, I'd always spot some rocker. Once, I noticed Ritchie Blackmore trying to comb his unruly hair while I was taking a pee.

One night, while drinking a Cadillac Margarita, to the right of me was English actor/comedy writer Marty Feldman, whom I talked with, sharing stories. He was full of laughter, and I must say, it was hard to look at him straight-on because of his misaligned eyes. But that was one of the things that made him so popular on television and in movies. He was hard to forget.

Also in the crowd you'd usually spot Quiet Riot, who frequented there, as well as Motorhead's entourage and Alice Cooper, whom I've seen plenty of times. One of his bandmates, guitarist Glen Buxton, was actually at our show when we played at the Starwood.

Our band always ran into Michael Des Barres and Nigel Harrison from Silverhead; also, the Dead Boys and The Runaways. Nigel joined Blondie later on and played bass for them for a while. Michael moved on as a lead vocalist for Power Station, replacing Robert Palmer, then went on to play for Detective. Desbarre moved on to acting in television and movies. He's noted for being a regular on the TV show MacGyver.

It was a cool time back then. The California music scene was pretty diverse. Glam, punk, power pop, gothic rock, heavy metal, heavy rock, and progressive rock were all popular at that same time period.

Speaking of the Runaways, I was friends with Jackie Fox, their bass player. She lived in the San Fernando Valley at that time, not too far away from my mother's home in Woodland Hills. One afternoon she brought over the whole band: Sandy West, Joan Jett, Lita Ford and Cherie Curie! On that day, I gave Sandy my leather jacket with studded red jewels.

"Are you sure I can have this?" she asked me.

"It's too small for me now," I told her. "It's from my days playing with the Motor City Bad Boys."

She put it on and said, "It fits perfect! Wow, thanks!" Then she hugged me. I really miss her. Sadly, she passed away in 2006 at only forty-seven from lung cancer.

Lita wanted to try on my snakeskin pants, so I said, "Okay, you can try them on in the other room."

My brother, Kenny, was home and took a quick peek, then laughed out loud. She had split open the rear seams of my pants by accident. They were custom made out of this patent leather kind of material, but I never suspected that would happen! Don't think I ever wore them again after that. I was really pissed. Well, you win some, you lose some.

Before leaving, all the girls signed my copy of their debut album and said thanks.

When it was time to take promotional photos of the Killer Kane Band, our manager, William Forney, would plan out each location. In the San Fernando Valley was this place called Sherman Oaks Castle Park. It was a family amusement park with batting cages, arcade games and three miniature-golf courses. He took several photos there. While we were hanging outside for the photo shoot, Mickey Dolenz and Peter Tork were walking with their kids towards us. It was funny seeing half of the Monkees, a band I've always been quite fond of, especially their syndicated comedy TV show.

At another location in Los Angeles, more photos were taken for a few magazines with our heads being served on a silver platter. This was an idea Blackie had in mind that came to life.

On September 10th 1975, we recorded three songs that were eventually pressed on 7" vinyl. The New York label, Whiplash Records, put it out. This label was one of the first devoted to punk and other related genres. "Don't Need You," "Long Haired Woman," and "Mr. Cool" were finished late that evening in some Los Angeles Recording Studio that I just can't remember. Even my master tape reel does not indicate where we were!

By the way, the song "Mr. Cool" reappeared just years later as the heavy-metal band W.A.S.P.'s "Cries in the Night." This led to a lawsuit with Arthur and Blackie! (Note: The original version of "Mr. Cool" has been highly regarded as an influence to many upcoming artists around that time period, and it has been said that it sounds much better than the revamped version in structure, lyrics and guitar solos.

Killer Kane Band played a handful of gigs around town. The top gig, without a doubt, was our show in 1976, at The Starwood Club. Located smack dab in the middle of Hollywood at the intersection of Santa Monica Blvd and Crescent Heights. This club served as the stomping grounds for many other notable bands. Van Halen got their start there. Others who played there included Cheap Trick, Motley Crue, Quiet Riot, Black Flag, Devo, The Damned, The Runaways, The Motels, The Dead Boys, The Jam, The Ramones, The Go Go's, and The Knack.

Our band played top bill at The Starwood with The Hollywood Stars and Ron Ashton's New Order. Poor Arthur was having problems handling his alcohol during this time and was struggling on stage that night. Just as we were setting up our equipment, he yelled, "Someone plug me in!" I freaked out and didn't know what to do, but thankfully Blackie took care of the situation and we were ready to take off.

Situated on the stage was a custom-made life-sized jail prop that Blackie jumped out of spitting fake blood into the audience up front. He was very theatrical and held the crowd's attention, that's for sure. As for me, I just concentrated on playing my best, no matter what. When looking out at the audience from time to time, I thought to myself, *Holy Shit! This place is packed!*

At one point during our show, the P.A. system blanked out and Blackie's vocals dropped. He got furious at the sound guy; you should have seen the look of rage on his face. We also had a prerecorded looped tape running in the background that got all tangled up. It was fixed, but almost too late! Finally, we finished playing our whole set, then played one short encore of a few cover songs.

After our set, we walked upstairs to our dressing room. My girlfriend was sitting on the couch waiting for me. To this day, I vividly remember everything that happened.

The backstage was packed with people. Lead guitarist from Y&T, Dave Meniketti, came up to me and said he loved the show and dug my guitar playing. I was shocked, considering he was and still is one Helluva fine guitarist. Kim Fowley, D.J. Rodney Bingenheimer, Glen Buxton, Ron Ashton and Dennis Thompson were all backstage hanging out and drinking with us. After all these years, I still have the original sign welcoming the Killer Kane Band that was scotch-taped to our dressing room door.

After we played, our roadies found all sorts of crazy shit— girls' bra's, girl's phone numbers written in lipstick on paper napkins, and broken glass beer bottles. Looking back, I would say it was a fire hazard with occupancy exceeding the limit of this club. I'm glad there was no fire that night!

This gal who worked for *The Star*, an adult trade magazine, wrote a review stating that the decadent glitter-crowd in the audience were non-appreciative. The Starwood Club was closed down in 1981 due to underage drinking citations and noise abatement issues, plus a whole mess of more violations.

Speaking of violations, one night when I was upstairs on the balcony checking out a new band, The Damned were upstairs as well, hanging out and drinking. I remember Rat Scabies was throwing Heineken glass beer bottles straight out into the crowd downstairs.

I told him, "What the fuck man? You're gonna get us kicked out of here, you idiot!"

He just laughed. My God, he was so pathetically bloody drunk. Right before things could get any worse, I got the hell out of there.

Here's a little bit of history about the Starwood. It was managed by Elmer Valentine, the founder of the Whiskey a Go-Go. Prior to becoming the Starwood, it was a very popular jazz club called P.J.'s. In the 1960's, The Bobby Fuller Four, The Standells, Trini Lopez and The Buddy Rich Band recorded live albums there. Around 1972, P.J.'s was bought by organized crime figure Eddie Nash who closed then re-opened the place as the Starwood. Here are some known facts about Nash: In the 1970's, he was one of the wealthiest and most dangerous gangster's operating on the West Coast.

Another gig that Killer Kane played was on October 9th, 1975, at Myron's Ballroom for an even larger crowd. Once again, we headlined. The other bands that played were the Berlin Brats and Dragon. The Berlin Brats later changed their name to the Mau Maus. This concert was held during the week, and once again, the place was packed. This crowd was wild, unruly and terribly disruptive. Arthur and Blackie, from what I heard after the show, got into a squabble about something and were involved in a fight with a bunch of punks outside of the venue. I never really got the whole truth to the story about that night. Thankfully, no one ended up in the hospital. Honestly, that gig could be best described as a rock 'n' roll romper room. As it turned out, an old friend from my childhood days in New York ran backstage asking for me. I asked our roadie who it was.

He yelled, "Steven Hoffman."

I yelled back, "Let him in!"

Wow, hadn't seen Steve in over eight years. It was weird. He was visiting Los Angeles from Miami Beach, Florida, and flipped out when he heard I was playing in this band. He was very excited to see me. It was great to see him again too! Unfortunately, that was the last time we ever spent time together reminiscing. He passed away not long ago, on September 15th 2018. I'm filled with complete sadness, that we never got back in touch from that day on.

Word sure spread about that Myron's Ballroom gig. Flyers were posted all over Hollywood. Surprisingly, several photos of Bruce Springsteen showed up just by chance, standing right next to one of our flyers pasted on a post when he was in town promoting his *Born to Run* album. These photos of Bruce have been circulated all over the internet. As a matter of fact, one of those photos is on the front cover of the book, *The Stories Behind the Songs*, by Brian Hiatt.

We played many other gigs, and some were a bit different, such as playing a special show at the Ambassador Hotel. It felt a bit strange, given the fact that in the room where we were setting up, on June 5th 1968, presidential candidate Robert F. Kennedy was fatally shot by Sirhan Sirhan. Things went well, but boy it sure felt a bit eerie to me.

Another gig we played was at a small bar in Venice, California, called The Old Sundown Saloon. It was on September 17th, 1975. We just about got thrown out because of playing too loud for such a small venue and leaving a big mess on stage. People were so close to the stage that I felt a bit uneasy.

We received a few letters from record labels. One recording studio, Dynamic Recording, wrote us a letter that I kept and I'll quote:

> Dear Killer Kane,
> Thank you for the privilege of being your guest at the Sundown Saloon Show September 17. You played the same fucking shit I've heard the last 10 years. You play too loud, your show was extremely rude, you had no respect for the audience, you drink too much and WE LOVE YOU. Wishing you the very best of luck in the future.
> I remain:
> Sincerely,
> Roy McMillan

There were several rock magazines that wrote about us. Many critics described The Killer Kane Band as gritty, Alice Cooper-styled proto-punk type of music. Well, whatever. At that gig, we played a few cover tunes: "Stranded in the Jungle," originally recorded by the Cadets, played New York Dolls style, and Ricky Nelson's "Poor Little Fool," which Arthur sang in his most unusual voice. He handed me his bass guitar, then told me to play along, which I did, backing him up while Blackie played rhythm guitar.

When Arthur stepped up on that stage, I couldn't believe it! Arthur was in very rare form that night, just wailing away. A very rare moment indeed! He wore his notorious red, patent-leather jumpsuit, which was previously worn when The New York Dolls, all dressed up in red patent-leather for their last shows at The

Little Hippodrome Club in New York. They decorated the club in a faux-communist red theme. At that point, they were managed by Malcolm McLaren. It was his idea to dress up their show that way.

Moving on, in the summer of 1979, I received a phone call from The Dead Boys road manager, James, that The Ramones invited The Dead Boys and Killer Kane Band to the premier screening of their movie, "Rock 'N Roll High School," in Hollywood. With that kind of offer, I told him of course we'd be there! We wouldn't miss it for the world!

I drove out to meet up with my bandmates outside the movie theatre. Honestly, I just can't remember that theater's name, but from what I recall, it was not too far away from The Tropicana Hotel, where the Ramones were staying. That was Santa Monica Blvd. in West Hollywood. When we were getting seated, to the right of me was Stiv Bators, lead vocalist from the Dead Boys, who later hooked up with The Lords of the New Church. To the left of me was Joey Ramone (lead vocalist from you know who!). In that same row were Blackie and Arthur from my band and next to them were The Rubber City Rebels. Both bands recorded on the Sire Records label, as well as also being from Akron and Cleveland, Ohio.

Before the movie started, out of the blue, I asked Joey if I could try on his sunglasses. He asked me why. I told him they looked really cool and just wondering what kinda tint they were. When I looked at how thick those lenses were, "I yelled Holy Shit! You're practically blind!" I had no idea they were prescription sunglasses.

He then said, "Gimme them back, you Fuck!" OMG. He was so pissed off! Right after that moment, Stiv asked me how to get rid of crabs. That's when I realized we were all complete morons.

I told this story to Arturo Vega, years later, before he passed away in 2013. Arturo worked with the Ramones right from their very start. He was a graphic designer and created many of the band's logos, including their "Hey Ho, Let's Go," which mocked the U.S. presidential shield. He was very involved with the band as their artistic director and lighting and stage director. He was also virtually considered the fifth member of The Ramones. He told me, "Look, just dedicate your book to me and the boys. I totally believe you. You were always nuts and a real wise guy." So sad. I still have his email address and phone number in my computer files.

Anyway, after the movie was over there was a little party. Some of the actors were there hanging out with us: P.J. Soles, Mary Woronov, Paul Bartel and Clint Howard. Those are a few that I can remember.

As I'm writing this book, what really makes me sad is all four of the original Ramones have passed away, including Arturo. Things will never be the same again. The music world will never be the same again. Just glad I've seen them perform live plenty of times during their heyday.

At another event in early March 1976, I received two complimentary tickets to see Paul Kossoff and Back Street Crawler at The Starwood. Funny . . . Killer Kane had played on that very same stage just months before. I brought my brother with me to the show that evening. D.J. Rodney Bingenheimer introduced the band.

After about fifteen minutes or so, my brother and I noticed Paul swaying back and forth like he was drunk or very high. After a few songs, he looked really weak—so much so that it was scary! As the show continued, we were happy to see his old bandmates— vocalist Paul Rodgers, drummer Simon Kirke, bassist Boz Burrell, and even guitarist Mick Ralphs (better known as the band Bad Company)—joining him on stage. But as the show progressed, Paul was fading out. When we were driving home that night, we talked about how he looked all strung out. Just weeks later, we heard the sad news. He died on March 19th, 1976. Such a brilliant guitarist, especially when he played with the band, Free. I'll never forget that strange night.

Well, living in the San Fernando Valley, it sure was more relaxed than Hollywood. Total suburbia. Many actors, celebrities and musicians chose to reside there as it was not far from the city but still close enough to drive in for meetings and auditions. There was this popular local deli in Encino named Fromin's, located on Ventura Boulevard. Every other weekend I'd go there and pick up assorted bagels, cream cheese, smoked salmon, corned beef and pastrami sandwiches, rugelach, and other pastries for my mom, brother, sister and me. Every time I went it was busy. One given Saturday morning, upon arrival, I noticed rocker Tom Petty walking in with his stepson.

I said, "Hey, Tom Petty! What's new?"

He looked at me kind of funny, then said, "Hey, man," and his kid waved.

We both basically placed our orders at the same time. All of a sudden, his order was ready and I was still waiting. As a matter of fact, I was waiting for a pretty long time, so I had to ask, "Where the heck is my order?"

The dude behind counter responded and asked me, "Hey do you know who that was you were talking to?"

I responded, "Hell, yeah! Where's my order?"

Finally, it came. Guess I ordered too much.

Yeah, in the San Fernando Valley, more than in Hollywood, from time to time you most likely will spot someone that you recognize from television or in the music world. A great example of that is the time my family got invited over for dinner at my Aunt Isabel and Uncle Joel's home. They lived in Encino, right up the hill from the Jackson family home off of Hayvenhurst Boulevard. Sometimes I had to drive another route to get to Encino Hills Drive from Mulholland Drive because of all the fans hoping to get a glimpse of Michael Jackson.

It was raining that night. I stopped off beforehand at the local newsstand to pick up a copy of *Rolling Stone* magazine. When I looked up, standing right in front of me was, you guessed it, Michael Jackson! He was surprisingly tall. All I said was, "Oh, hello, Michael." He looked at me, then he ran off with his coat over his head. That was so weird. Can you imagine? Even back then he was extremely cautious about any encounter with someone he did not know.

In the San Fernando Valley, Balboa Park was a very popular place to take your kids, walk your dog, or play football, baseball and soccer. My brother and I would play basketball there on the weekends. Sometimes, Michael's brother, Jackie, would play with us. Other times, you never knew who'd show up.

It was really bad in the 1970's as far as the severe smoggy weather we had living in the valley. We'd have to rest every so often as the air was so thick, our lungs felt heavy. My brother had asthma, which only made it worse. When sitting down relaxing one afternoon, I noticed actor Al Lewis sitting on a bench near me. This I couldn't figure? But then I realized he was just there watching his grandson play ball. Al was most notable for playing "Grandpa" on the TV Series *The Munsters*. I had to say hello. He was nice and a pleasure to talk to. What a cool memory.

One minute later, right over my shoulder, I noticed Sergio Mendes walking his little chihuahua. It was hilarious. Just your typical star sighting, I figured.

As to the short life of The Killer Kane Band, which lasted just a couple of years, we attended many a venture in the local music circuit. It was around December 1975 when Arthur and our band were invited to see Mott the Hoople perform at the Los Angeles Forum. Overend Watts, their bass player, was good friends with Arthur. Interestingly, his personality traits were like Arthur's gentle, mellow personality.

After their gig with Aerosmith and Montrose, we met up at the Forum Club for an after-party. Many celebrities and a few former bandmates from Mott were present backstage. At this point, Ray Major was playing lead guitar with Mott. However, I bumped into guitarist Ariel Bender. The greatest experience for me was sharing a pint of beer with Ariel, aka Luther Grosvenor. He also played guitar with Spooky Tooth, one of my favorite bands from England. He had replaced Mick Ralphs, Mott's original guitarist. For me, this was by far the coolest thing . . . simply chatting about Spooky Tooth, their lead vocalist Mike Harrison, and keyboardist Gary Wright. We talked about guitars and all sorts of stuff. Couldn't believe I was sitting next to him, just hanging out. Being a huge fan growing up, it was just awesome.

Well, Sadly, The Killer Kane Band broke up due to many factors which I'll just leave up to your imagination.

On another sad note—and this applies to Arthur—on July 13th, 2004, Arthur Harold Kane Jr., my dear old friend, bandmate and former New York Dolls bass player, passed away from leukemia at the age of fifty-five. About a week before his passing, he was complaining about what he thought was a bad case of the flu. Unfortunately, it turned out to be much more serious. On a happy note, he did have the chance to reunite with his old remaining bandmates from the New York Dolls, David Johansen and Syl Sylvain, at Morrisey's Meltdown Festival in London just one month before his passing. This made him feel happy and appreciated. He was a good friend, soft-spoken, and a genuinely nice guy with a gentle soul. He had this crazy, cool wardrobe of clothes stored in his closet. Most of that stuff was from his New York Dolls days. I'd visit him in his Hollywood apartment every so often. I believe it was called the Nirvana Building. It was located around the corner from the historic Magic Castle. Barbara, his girlfriend, was living with him at the time. This was just a couple of years before they got married. We had many fun conversations and there was always something going on.

One day, Robert "Buffalo" Roberts was there hanging out. He played saxophone in Frank Zappa's band, Ruben and The Jets, and was also a tattoo artist. He was their neighbor, living just a few doors away. We were eating Italian submarine sandwiches that we had delivered and were laughing and having a good time.

Then, on the spur of the moment, we talked about our favorite cartoon theme songs from the 1960's. Growing up in New York, Arthur and I loved watching cartoons. He told me the New York Dolls recorded the theme song to Courageous Cat and Minute Mouse and they played it live a few times in concert. He always enjoyed playing the intro bass line to that tune. Arthur gave me a few things to wear, like red suspenders and a white bicycle belt with flashing lights that Iggy Pop gave him, plus a few tee shirts that didn't fit him anymore.

Before any of our shows, we always traded clothes and told each other what looked good on each one of us. That basically goes for most any band as well. One of his t-shirts had perforated, puffy red letters spelling "Killer Kane" on a Kelly-green shirt. (This was when he played with the New York Dolls.) He wanted me to have it; I wish I still did. But I have a few photos in safe-keeping, as well as photos of Jerry and Syl wearing those same custom-made t-shirts. I miss him very much; and his funny laugh whenever I told him all my nutty jokes. A movie about his life came out on DVD called *New York Doll*. It came out a year after his death in 2005. It's certainly worth watching.

I was in-between jobs at that time; thinking to myself, *Jesus, I'm like a monkey in the middle, trying to decipher should I play in another band or seek work in the music industry?*

First, I auditioned for playing guitar in The Motels. It was strange, as I initially received a phone call from Martha Davis, their lead vocalist. She must have known someone who knew me. I was familiar with their songs, but never played them. I remember meeting her; she was nice and knew of the Killer Kane Band. But I had this feeling I just didn't fit in. The results? It didn't work out and just wasn't meant to be.

So, I continued hitting the club circuit and partied not far from home. Some weekends I'd drive to Hollywood, but there were plenty of places to go to in the San Fernando Valley. For example, The Country Club in Reseda and Perkins Palace in Pasadena had many cool shows happening at the time. The Palomino was another destination in North Hollywood if you wanted to see your cowpunk type of bands such as Lone Justice, Long Ryders, or The Blasters. Perkins was a bit of a drive, so I didn't go there much unless there was some major event I couldn't live without.

In Calabasas, The Sagebrush Cantina was an interesting change of pace. In the 1970's it was the place to meet girls and for girls to meet guys. You know this is leading up to another story.

Every other weekend, my friends and I would go to The

Sagebrush Cantina for food and drinks. One night I met a very pretty girl and we started talking. Nothing really happened until I met her again and she gave me her phone number. I called her weeks later to ask her out, but she told me she had just started dating a nice guy from England who played in a band. Out of curiosity, I asked her his name. She replied, "Jeff Lynne; he plays guitar."

I freaked! "You mean Jeff Lynne from E.L.O.?"

"Yes. How do you know?"

Well, that was enough for me. Right at that moment, I knew this phone conversation wasn't going to go anywhere. To make a long story short, weeks later she phoned me and said she was engaged. Wow, that was quick! Then, she invited me to her family's home for a pre-party celebration. Guess you're wondering her name? Sandi Kapelson.

So, off I went. Sure enough, there was Jeff Lynne offering me a pint of Foster's Beer. First time I ever drank Foster's, and it was refreshing. We shook hands, then met the rest of the band members. I had a great time and was offered some very tasty appetizers and the drinks kept on coming. Looking back, I just had to laugh. Little did Sandi know back then that I had followed Jeff Lynne's career from playing in Idle Race and The Move to E.L.O.

In the interim, work-wise, something interesting did come up. Just my luck, my sister's girlfriend's father was a comedy writer, producer and director. His name was Chris Bearde, best known for his work as a writer on *Rowan & Martin's Laugh-In* and for co-writing and producing television specials for Elvis Presley and Sonny & Cher in the 1960's. He had an opening for a production assistant on a new musical variety show that would be airing on NBC late night. The show pilot he was producing was called *Top Ten*, which was a satire on various aspects of life such as Top Ten songs and Charo's Top Ten most difficult words to pronounce. Pretty much an upbeat, fun, nutty show starring DJ Rick Dees and his wife Julie, plus Phil Hartman (*Saturday Night Live /Pee Wee's Playhouse*). So, I was hired! As this was my first time ever working in television, I had no idea what to expect.

My job dealt directly with record labels, personal managers, and production companies, receiving videotapes and promotional materials needed for the show. I also assisted celebrity stars on set. Each day was different, and I was on a call alert schedule for various projects. What I didn't know, though, were the other duties involved, like cleaning up the office and providing coffee for the production staff.

Jim Aubrey was the president of CBS Television at the time. His son, Jay Aubrey, told me to do many other things which I plainly refused. This got me into a bit of trouble with Chris.

Chris took me aside and said, "Hey, look, I'm sorry. I know Jay's a total *Ass!* But Jim Aubrey is the guy that's paying you each week. So, please, please, help me here, okay?"

Right after Chris left, I noticed Flo and Eddie were on the set looking at me and eavesdropping. They were also featured in a segment on this show. Both of them, in unison, asked, "Hi, Ajay! Can you bring us two cups of coffee with a few fresh pastries?"

I replied, "Screw you, guys!"

As much as I loved The Turtles and their vocal recordings with Marc Bolan and Zappa, they were two wise-asses. So, I went on with my day. Had to pick up Audrey and Judy Landers and drive them to Los Angeles Airport. They were two beautiful, blonde actresses who appeared on many television programs such as *Dallas, Charlie's Angels. Love Boat* and *The Dukes of Hazzard.* At least they were nice to me.

Ray Saluga was also on the show. He was a comedian best known for his, "You can call me Ray" routine. He appeared on the *Gong Show* frequently as a guest.

It was my first taste of television, and it wasn't as much fun as I imagined. Just like my first taste of live television on *Wonderama* when I was a kid didn't live up to expectations. An interesting experience, though. I still have the original script tucked away in a box. The show was cancelled. Never made it. There ya go.

Oh, almost forgot, let's take a trip backwards a bit to the summer of 1978. An old friend of my brother's growing up decided to move to California from New York. I hung out with his older brother, Gary, but was friends with him also. His name was Rocco, a hairstylist. His father owned a well-known beauty school in Manhattan called Robert Fiance. (To this day, business has expanded to many other locations, from New Jersey to Florida.) He rented a room from my mom briefly, then moved to Venice Beach. He worked at Vidal Sassoon for a while and a few other well-known salons in town. This guy was a bit crazy, and he partied a lot. Funny as hell, too! I attended many wild events with him.

All I can say is, never was there a dull moment. I can't forget the day when Rocco's friend Sue, a very pretty hairstylist with whom he worked with at the time, was dating Arnold Schwarzenegger. She invited both of us to join them to see the movie *Freaks*, a Tod Browning film from 1932. (This movie was banned in the United Kingdom for over thirty years!) A special screening was held at The NuArt Theatre on Santa Monica Boulevard.

To my surprise, after the movie was over Arnold talked to me. I was wearing a t-shirt and shorts. "You work out?" he asked in his Austrian-jock accent.

"Not with weights," I said.

"You have strong calves."

"Well, I play basketball, racquetball, and I'm really active," I said. It was pretty cool hearing that from Arnold, as he was so incredibly buff! Funny, who would have ever thought that years later, in 2003, after years as a huge movie star, Arnold Schwarzenegger would become Governor of California! He served until 2011.

Rocco & I must've been on a roll, because, just a few months later on September 24th 1978, one outrageously flamboyant event took place. It was by Special invite only and closed to the general public. Rocco called me ahead of time and said, "We're gonna crash a party. Just make sure you dress cool and stylish. Better wear a suit! Okay?"

"Okay!"

So, I drove out from the San Fernando Valley to Venice Beach. Turned out, it was a private party for renowned artist Andy Warhol and his *Interview* magazine. The party was held at a gay dinner club called Robert's, located right on the main strip of Venice Beach, California. After walking past Muscle Beach, street vendors, Hari Krishna's, and roller skaters, with the added stench of patchouli oil and musk incense flowing in the air, we finally arrived. Rocco was dressed up in a nice black suit with a colorful patterned shirt. I was also wearing a black suit, and to be honest, we both walked in like we owned the place. What we were about to discover was that we blended in perfectly, looking like rock stars.

The place was crowded that evening. Upon our first steps inside, we were both handed a copy of Andy Warhol's *Interview* magazine. Berry Berenson was featured on the front cover. She was married to actor Tony Perkins at the time. Apparently, she was at this party, but I did not see her. One thing I must mention that many people may not know: She died in the September 11 attacks as a passenger on American Airlines Flight #11, in 2001. She was only fifty-three years old. She was a beautiful model, actress and photographer. Sad story.

As we were walking through the front entrance, male servers were walking by with tasty exotic appetizers and drinks. They were topless, wearing a black bow tie around their neck and black slacks. The female servers were dressed almost the same. (God, wish they had been topless!) Kidding aside, the women servers were only wearing black bras with a black skirt and black, hi-heeled shoes. I looked at Rocco and he looked at me like, *Wow! This is the place to be brother!*

Many celebrities were present at this event. I spotted Pia Zadora right when I walked in. She was very pretty and so petite—only five feet tall!

As I was walking through to meet Andy Warhol, I spotted Ursula Andress. Oh, my God, a Bond girl! She looked absolutely gorgeous. I just had to meet her. So, I walked nervously up to her and said hello. To my surprise, she mistook me for someone else!

Then kissed me, then hugged me! I thought I was going to have a heart attack! That really caught me off-guard!

She said, "Marcello, how are you? Nice to see you."

I just played along remembering the time I was mistaken for Paul from KISS and how that turned out. This didn't go the same route, but still, it was surreal. I couldn't believe this was actually happening to me. It's a moment frozen in time. At that time, I had long black curly hair and was wearing a black suit, with an electric-blue dress shirt and pointy black Italian leather shoes.

Finally, I met Andy Warhol. He was sitting in the middle of a large round table with bodyguards on one side and beautiful women on the other side of him. (Andy had been shot and almost killed once, so that explained the bodyguards.)

I asked him if he would be kind enough to sign my Interview magazine, which he did with a black-felt marker. He wrote, "From one Andy to another Andy" and signed it, "Andy Warhol."

He was soft spoken and very composed. Certainly, an interesting person to talk to. His autograph now hangs on my wall in my office. Always prepared, Rocco then handed him two Campbell's Soup Cans which Andy signed. But, since Rocco moved many times, he lost those soup cans in the shuffle years later. As that night progressed, we ate and drank like kings. Gotta hand it to the Rock, we sure pulled off a winner!

That's a party I'll never forget. Robert's is now long gone. Wished I'd brought a camera with me that night. Oh well. FYI, there is a segment talking about this party in a book, *The Andy Warhol Diaries*, on p.172.

So, here's a story ending the 1970's and closing our Chapter Three. I don't remember the fucking month, but in 1979, I received a phone call from one of my old friends, Michael, with whom I grew up in Queens, New York. He had just moved to L.A. and happened to be friends with the band The Dickies. They stored their stage props in his warehouse in North Hollywood.

Since he was friends with Stan Lee, Leonard, Billy Club and Chuck Wagon, they invited both of us to one of their shows. It was at Perkins Palace in Pasadena. I'd just had surgery on my right foot, and, at that time, I was using crutches. We sat up front and went backstage after their set ended with passes the band provided. A huge commotion started when Leonard spit on the people in the orchestra pit. Those concert goers went crazy and rushed towards the stage. The backstage passes were only for after the concert ended. When the crowd went out of control, we asked the bouncer if he could let us go backstage, but he wouldn't until the set ended.

It really got nuts when the punks in front of the orchestra pit were slam dancing, and spitting up at Leonard while he was singing. He got mad and eventually whipped out his penis and pissed all over them. Right then and there, it set off a near riot!

Later, outside in the parking lot, those pissed-on punkers were hanging out, throwing various debris at the band. I felt sorry for anyone who happened to be in range. What a wild night that was. The end of an Era.

Chapter Four
Warner Elektra Atlantic Corp Years 1980's

So here we are; another decade! The 1980's! A very colorful period in the fashion world and the beginning of an empire called MTV. Twenty-four hours a day of music videos. Just what we needed. Now we have YouTube! But it was also a real fun time with all the happening things to do in the Hollywood/Los Angeles area.

There was one awesome street besides Sunset Boulevard. Melrose Avenue! At that time, the Melrose strip spread for miles and had many hip, trendy restaurants, boutique shops and plenty of independent record stores. A Thai food restaurant called Tommy Tangs was extremely popular, and usually long lines of people were just waiting to get in.

One weekend, my sister and her girlfriend, Wendy, joined me for dinner. While we were waiting for a table, I noticed actress/vocalist Michelle Phillips sitting right across from me reading an *L.A. Weekly* magazine. So, just out of the blue, I asked her if she could read me my horoscope. After she asked me what month I was born in and what my sign was, we got into a deep discussion. When we got up to be seated, my sister's girlfriend was looking at me in shock. I asked her what was the matter.

She said, "You are so cool! Do you know who that was?"

I replied, "Of course. Just treat celebrities like you would want to be treated, and be sincere."

Another interesting moment took place at L.A. Eyeworks, also located on Melrose Ave. One of the most sought-after destinations for an abundance of amazing designer frames and sunglasses. While shopping with my girlfriend, the number of cool shades to choose from was endless! I finally picked out two pairs, but didn't have enough money to get both. Suddenly, standing two feet away from me was Elton John.

I said, "Hello, Elton. Can you tell me which pair looks better on me?"

He said, "That pair your wearing fits you perfectly!"

I told him, "Thanks!"

My girlfriend was embarrassed and told me I was a nutcase. And that was the pair I brought home. Just so you know, Elton has literally spent thousands of dollars through the years at L.A. Eyeworks for custom-designed sunglasses.

While still living in the San Fernando Valley, I figured I'd give working in the record business a go. I applied for a job at Warner Elektra Atlantic Corporation (WEA Corp). Various positions were posted in the *Los Angeles Times* classified section. They opened a huge warehouse in Chatsworth, California, to stock their ever-growing catalog of recording artists. vinyl LPs, 7" vinyl, prerecorded cassette tapes and video tapes of music and movies.

I was hired and worked there from 1980–1985. During the first few years, I made a few friends. One of them was a nice girl named Linda. She was hip. Her hair was blonde, but I could tell she dyed it a lot. I forget her last name, but I remember it was of German descent. Anyway, she heard of my old band, Killer Kane, then told me she was friends with model Jerry Hall and was going to go on tour with her and the Rolling Stones in a couple of months. I said, "Get outta here"; I didn't believe her. She always dressed cool, though, and was pretty trendy. She also knew a lot about music and all the gossip surrounding rock celebrities at the time. She was quite crazy, too! One weekend, late at night, I received a phone call from the police, asking me if I knew her. I asked what happened. Then I told the officer, "She works with me."

He replied, "She was driving her BMW on three wheels and sparks were flying off the highway."

I had heard a lot in my day, but this stunned me into silence.

"Plus," the cop added, "she was way above the drinking limit for alcohol and on the wrong side of the road."

He put her on the phone to speak with me. She was crying profusely and asked me if I could help her as she didn't want her parents to know what had just happened. She apparently came from a wealthy family. The bail was set at $500, and then she would have to go to court. I didn't have that kind of money on hand, but I could use my credit card to get her out. She promised to pay me back, which she did. What a mess! A few months after that incident she said,

"Hey, so I'm going on that Stones tour soon and won't be coming back to work. But I'll call you when I get back home."

Even though I understood, I still didn't believe her. Just in case, I gave her two Rolling Stones books I had laying around. One was a tour book, the other was a history book with many cool photos. I asked her if they could be signed by Keith and Mick. She said no problem.

A few months later, I received a phone call from her. We met for lunch and she handed me back my books. To my surprise, many pages were missing and ripped out of both books! As I was scrolling through, many were signed by Mick Jagger and Keith Richards with their thoughts on photos plus other notes such as to Brian Jones's death, which freaked me out.

Mick wrote, "Bloody fool, he killed himself," in big letters, meaning Brian committed suicide! Looking back, wish I hadn't sold those books, but years later after losing my job, I needed the money. They were eventually sold to Rockaway Records Collectibles in Los Angeles more than twenty-five years ago.

The story about Brian's death is still debated to this day. My thoughts are, it was a cover up. Well, during our lives many of us have, at some point, done stupid things that we later regret. All you could do is learn a lesson and move on. Yeah, guess you can say in today's market, those books would appear as rare collectibles in your typical rock auction and raise big money.

♪♫♪

1982 was an interesting year because that's when compact disc digital audio arrived. But we'll get back to that format in a little bit.

My job at W.E.A. Corp started out in the checking and packing department. Basically, I learned all facets of warehouse distribution. After a while, I was advanced to the Promo/ Marketing department. where I was responsible for the distribution of all promotional merchandise and D.J. mailings of nationwide LP and singles releases, including Warner Home Video, on a weekly basis. Knowledge of all post office procedures was required, which I was trained for, and I ran the company mail. This was the position every employee wanted for various reasons. Two of us were working in that department. The other fellow acquired his job from his stepdad, who was a big shot at Atlantic Records. (This kind of thing was typical in the industry.) He was a nice guy, though, and we did get along and become friends.

The W.E.A. warehouse had about seventy-five or so people working there. The building had two floors: Accounting, Order Clerks, Customer Service and Returns Department were on the first floor; Sales Office and Corporate Staff were on the second floor. The place was enormous. Never in my life had I seen so much product. Stacks upon stacks of vinyl LPs were stored low and high up on the rafters. The stock seemed endless. So many formats: cassette tapes, videotapes, and box sets.

By the end of the week, almost every Friday, my department would hand out promo LP's, cassettes, posters, stickers, pinback buttons, and sometimes videotapes of music and movies to warehouse and office employees. Even the department in which I worked had stacks of vinyl LPs stored in bins and on wooden skids. Also, tons of posters, cardboard standees of associated artists, and movies as well. We even stored a few of Tower Records' large, painted store pieces that would be placed outside of their building promoting new releases per record label. One of them was Van Halen's 1984 album that was plastered up at their Sunset Boulevard location in Hollywood. When that album and promotion was over with, it was stored in our department.

The following week, my boss asked me if I wanted it. I asked him, where the heck would I be able to keep it? It looks cool, but I live in an apartment. I'll never forget the first day I worked in the promo department. My boss, who was the merchandising manager, told me and my partner to clean up the whole place, straighten things up, sweep the floors, take inventory and alphabetize everything in stock for easy access. Then, when all done, he said, "Hey, guys, feel free to take all the vinyl, posters, and standups you want, as we're gearing up for newly signed artists and more very soon!"

I literally went fucking crazy, grabbing the bands I liked from A to Z. A lot of stock was old but untouched. I searched through hundreds and hundreds of vinyl. First ultra-cool find was an original, rare pressing of the GTO's Permanent *Damage* LP with a gatefold sleeve and booklet on Straight Records from 1969. Frank Zappa produced that album. Also spotted a promotional Jimi Hendrix original Christmas 12". Around the corner were many promotional cardboard standees. I picked up a Neil Young standee that lit up when plugged in, promoting his *Decade* 2 record set; a Rod Stewart standee from *Foolish Behavior*; Frank Sinatra standee from *L.A. Is My Lady*; and a Richard Pryor *Live on the Sunset Strip* standee. Just to give you an idea, my whole car was filled up with promo goodies. So, to be safe and smart, I waited until everyone else went home that evening. Not only would jealousy occur; if they loved music, they would be so angry for what my co-worker Randy and I brought home that night.

From the years 1980–1985, I gained the knowledge and experience for successfully working in this business and a vast collection of recorded music formats. So, let's talk about what went on in my department those years! Many artists would come by to visit and sign autographs on their latest release, and, in some cases, we would be treated to a listening party luncheon for all employees. Just a quick rundown on the bands and solo artists that visited W.E.A. through those years: Loudness, Bootsy Collins, George Duke, Larry Carlton, Joe Walsh, Todd Rundgren, Robert Fripp (King Crimson), Jim Capaldi (Traffic), Josie Cotton, Berlin, The Blasters, Van Halen, Metallica, and

Paul Barrere (Little Feet). Part of my job was simply to setup tables with a stack of promotional LP copies of the solo artist or band that would be visiting that day.

Usually, we would have a meet-and-greet session with the artist, and a signing afterwards. Things went well most of the time . . . except once. Quite an interesting thing happened when I had extra promo copies of This Mortal Coil's debut LP, *It'll End in Tears*. It was on the Valentino Label, a sublabel of Atco Records, which released the album in late 1984. This was the only time a This Mortal Coil album was released simultaneously in the U.K. and in the U.S.A. No one picked up any of the twenty-five albums sitting on that table! Not one. They were free, for God's sake! If people only knew how big the cult following would become for this album and, furthermore, the 4AD label, they would regret it, especially as that copy is now a collector's item. Those twenty-five vinyl records were to be placed on a wooden skid then melted down and destroyed when promotion was over, just like many others. Managers at independent stores and D.J.'s had already received their copies.

To this day, I still cannot grasp the act of melting down vinyl. Same thing regarding posters. I remember when Foreigner's *Provocateur* album promotion ended. I was asked to shred all remaining posters left over. There was a stack of two hundred leftover, and they were shredded. That kind of made sense to me, but not a playable piece of work. Those days, working in the distribution business was nutty. Oh, regarding those *This Mortal Coil* LP's, I took a handful home and gave them to my good friends. When Jim Capaldi came by to visit, promoting his *Fierce Heart* album, he dropped by my department to say hello.

First thing I asked him while shaking his hand was, "How did Chris Wood die?"

I smelled liquor on his breath. It was, like, 11:00 mid-morning and I found that a bit strange. However, I am quite sure my question was just as strange.

Well, it didn't bother him one bit. He asked me, "Do ya have time mate?"

"I'll be working here all day to 5:00 p.m.," I said.

"Sit down, I'll tell you what really happened."

Being a huge fan of Traffic, I just had to know.

"Believe it or not," he said, "Chris Wood was the most talented musician in the band. A multi-instrumentalist! Even though known for playing flute and saxophone, he could play just about anything he got his hands on."

After a moment, Jim added, "Chris died from alcohol poisoning. Bootleg liquor."

That was really sad to hear. It is official record that, in 1983, Chris Wood died from pneumonia. But I totally believed Jim, and how could I not? We talked about music for a long time. When I looked at the clock, I noticed we had talked for almost an hour. Then I noticed my manager walking down the stairs.

"Hey get back to work!" he yelled at me.

"Who's that wanker?" Jim Capaldi asked.

"That's my boss," I said.

I shook his hand, quickly thanked him for the time we had just spent together, and got back to work. I'll never forget that afternoon, especially for everything he shared with me. I couldn't believe I was hanging out with a band member from Traffic, one of my favorite English bands of all time.

When Todd Rundgren came by, it was for his *A Cappella* album release. This was around 1985. As usual, I setup a long table with about a hundred stamped, promotional LP copies to give out to employees. A few hard-core fans of Todd brought several of his album jackets, hoping to have him sign that day. He was very cool, writing away and briefly talking to many people.

One woman I'll never forget, as she loved Todd so much, but was very nervous to meet him. She asked me politely if I could have him autograph a copy of *A Cappella* for her. I told her not to worry, everything would be fine. Sure enough, when she finally got to meet him after waiting in a long line, she froze.

"What's your name?" he asked her. She was speechless. Her mouth opened with no words coming out. I immediately stepped in.

"Her name is Debbie," I told Todd. "Please write something nice. Obviously, she's a big fan of yours."

He knew exactly what was going on and wrote a nice note to her accordingly. She thanked me later that day.

Well, being a guitarist, I had to ask Todd how he managed to obtain Eric Clapton's Gibson SG custom-painted guitar. He told me it was a gift from Eric.

"I hate you!" I joked. He laughed and said he purchased it back in the 1970's. He signed a nice photo playing that guitar which I brought with me from an old Circus magazine.

True story: George Harrison, after commissioning the paint job to artist Ed Roman in the mid-1960's gave the original guitar to his buddy Eric Clapton. It was a 1961 Gibson SG and was called "The Fool." Todd was cool and laughed with all the crazy shit I had to say about his recordings up to that period. I told him, in my opinion, *Something/Anything?* was his greatest achievement. He kind of agreed. We talked for a bit about his earlier recordings all the way to his first band, The Nazz. Before he left that day, he signed a whole bunch of stuff for me. I knew beforehand he was coming to visit, so I was prepared ahead of time. Really a nice guy.

The day Robert Fripp dropped by; I was completely blown away. I had a great time talking with Sir Robert about his days playing with King Crimson and his wife, Toyah. I even asked him about all his pedals he had on stage and what they were used for. He explained each one in detail, as well as his Frippertronics tape-looping technique. My God! What a long answer to my question. The way he spoke about each gadget and switch was like a scientist teaching his students. Honestly, it was so complex, my head was spinning.

He was promoting King Crimson's *Discipline* album. Photos were taken later that day in my department with WEA's warehouse manager, me, my coworker Randy and, of course, Robert. I'm so grateful he shared his life with me. Seriously, we talked about all the music up to that time frame, from albums *In the Court of the Crimson King* and *Lizard* to *Larks' Tongues in Aspic*, and *Starless and Bible Black*. He was a gentleman and one of the nicest musicians I've ever met. I'll never forget that day.

During my five-year tenure, we had many contests, listening luncheons, parties, live shows, and special visitors. One such as Richard Simmons, flamboyant fitness guru, actor and comedian. He was promoting his *Reach* album on Elektra Records in 1983. In his wacky, bossy, energetic tone, he made the whole warehouse of employees join him on his exercise routine while his album was playing on this kooky portable boom box. He put in a prerecorded cassette tape and off he went! It was one crazy scene! By far, the most obnoxious person I think I've ever met. Funny thing, there was speculation at that time (and even today) about his sexuality. But he has never discussed it.

One of the biggest promotions that I can remember was when Prince's *Purple Rain* album came out. This was a huge deal. In my department we had about seventy-five copies or so of the LP pressed in purple-colored vinyl, which we mailed out to a printed list of managers at Tower Records and other larger independent record stores. This was in June of 1984. We also stocked and sent out the following to retail music stores: Promotional Prince *Purple Rain* movie video tapes; vinyl lp's pinback buttons; posters; limited quantities of a promotional only *Purple Rain* umbrella; and a large cardboard standup of Prince sitting on his motorcycle from the movie soundtrack. That was such a busy time, the branch manager had his son work with us to make sure everyone got their packages on the street date of release.

One thing I need to mention is that, around this time, Warner Brothers in Burbank needed to store a whole lot of metal-cased master tape reels at our warehouse. The reason was that the heavy rains that year caused a leakage in their storage units. Upon further investigation, they could not afford the risk of water damage to their product. So, my coworker and I watched one section of the San Fernando W.E.A. warehouse being stocked by two workers, their product was placed on metal racks in a fenced area. It was a massive amount of stuff and was placed carefully side by side to each other. This stock was kept for a couple of months or so, and protected by an armed security guard. He was an older dude, like in his mid-60's. Even though the gate was locked up, this guard would stand by and sometimes sit down by the front entry during business hours. It was wild seeing this.

So, one day I noticed the door was open and the security guard was not present. I whispered to my coworker, "Hey, Let's check out this stuff!"

He whispered back, "Dude, we'll get in trouble. He's probably in the bathroom."

I said, "We're not stealing anything! We're just looking."

Well, we walked in and noticed the tapes were set up alphabetically by artist. I figured, let's just see what's stored on Jimi Hendrix and get the fuck outta here quickly. When we saw all the freaking tapes on Hendrix, we almost died. Holy Shit! It was so much stuff. Titles we had never seen before! We both figured it was enough music for the general public to hear for decades to come. We both looked at each other in amazement!

My coworker forgot we were whispering, "Dude this is THE HOLY GRAIL!"

Just as we were leaving, that guard noticed us, "Hey! What are you guys doing in here?

"Nothing really," I said.

"Just wondering what bands are being stored," my coworker said.

Thank God, nothing happened. We went back to work wondering if, maybe someday in the future, we would be able to hear those unreleased recordings. That day was certainly an experience for both of us to remember.

During my five years working at W.E.A. Corporation, I had many friends that worked for other record labels such as Capitol, MCA, Polygram and Columbia. Back then, we traded promo LP's every so often. A woman named Elsie worked with me for a while at W.E.A., but left to work for MCA. She got me in to enjoy many shows, which I was so thankful for. She was a good friend.

In the 1980's, so many cool alternative bands gave live performances. Transvision Vamp was one of them. I was invited backstage after their show at The Hollywood Palace. There I was, drinking with Wendy and her band, laughing and having a good time. The Buzzcocks were next door in another dressing room. It was a fun show with both bands.

Kim Wilde was very popular at that time and had a big hit, "Kids in America." I met her as well that night. She was so beautiful; I didn't know what to say but hello. She smiled and that was it.

I received many free concert tickets through those years working for W.E.A. Corp. In no special order, I got fantastic seats to see The Firm (featuring Jimmy Page and Paul Rodgers), INXS, Kraftwerk, Robert Palmer, Devo, Thin Lizzy, Howard Jones, Berlin, The Rolling Stones, The Blasters, Mink De Ville, Peter Tosh, and Dennis Brown. The best gift I ever received though, was from Mr. Brent Gordon who, at that time, was the Regional Vice President of Sales and Distribution and Marketing Operations. He did tell me that before giving me this special event pass, "I *do* expect you to be at work tomorrow on time. Okay?"

I promised. It was an event I'll never ever forget: Frankie Goes to Hollywood was having a special, private, invite-only party celebrating the release of *Welcome to The Pleasuredome*. This event was held in 1984 at the famous Hollywood Athletic Club, located at 6525 Sunset Boulevard—a landmark of a place with quite a history! It was built and commissioned in 1924 by Meyer & Holler. Architecture enthusiasts should find this of interest: Meyer & Holler were famous for building Grauman's Egyptian and Chinese Theatres. Charlie Chaplin, Rudolph Valentino and Cecil B. DeMille were the original founders of the Athletic Club. It has had a varied history through the years as a health club, bar, music venue and billiard room. During its heyday as a health club, members included Walt Disney, John Wayne, Humphrey Bogart, Jean Harlow, Clark Gable, Mae West and Howard Hughes.

However, during the mid-1980's, it was known as the Berwin Entertainment Complex. Many famous parties took place there.

David Geffen, Maxim's of Paris, and Princess Stephanie of Monaco all came to that building inquiring about renting out space for studios and clubs. Well, this party extravaganza was held smack in the middle of the week. Upon entering through the front doors, to my astonishment, the whole place was packed like canned sardines. You couldn't even move an inch without saying, Excuse me . . . *Twice!*

Frankie t-shirts were given out to each guest. Each one was different. Frankie Says Relax, Frankie Says War, and Frankie Says Relax Don't Do It. Unlimited alcohol was served all night. The lines for that alone were Totally insane. Hors d'oeuvres were served by waiters and waitresses walking around the club.

As I managed to ease myself through all these lovely people, I heard weird music playing, but it wasn't Frankie; it was an organ grinder with a freakin' monkey on top of his shoulders. He was an old man; his appearance was similar to that of a traveling gypsy. I thought I was hallucinating. But at that point I had only downed a couple of beers. A popcorn machine was running next to him. Then, to my surprise, of all the people in the world, Nina Hagen and Angelyne were standing right in front of me! OMG!

Angelyne's breasts popped right out of her top in my face! She was on billboards all around Los Angeles at that time and had a cult following as a singer, actress and model.

Nina Hagen though . . . Jesus!

Seeing them together, it was double gonzo!

But it does make sense to me now that I think about it. For some of you who may not know, Nina Hagen is a German singer, songwriter and actress known for her theatrical stage presence and over-the-top vocals. She was an Iconic figure during the Punk and New Wave scene in late 1970's and early 1980's. I didn't quite know what to say to these two hotties! So, without hesitation said, "I Love you girls. You're the most beautiful creatures in the Hollywood Kingdom!"

Angelyne said, "Thank you," and smiled politely.

Nina Hagen yelled, "Oh, fuck off!"

I looked at her, said, "Okay," then walked away.

She scared me.

After a while I was getting very drunk. Free booze? Unheard of! Phoned every one of my friends that evening to come out and meet me, but it was a weeknight, and many had to work the following morning. Their loss, I guess. Moving through the massive crowd once again, walking down a long hallway. Finally, on a small stage, Frankie Goes to Hollywood starting playing. Holly Johnson was in top form and the band sounded fantastic.

The next morning, as expected, I was hung over and felt like total crap the whole damn day. But it was worth it.

Another cool private party I attended was for Van Halen. It was held at A&M Studios in Hollywood on La Brea Avenue. It was right around when their album *1984* came out. I brought my girlfriend with me, who at that time, loved David Lee Roth. Yeah, she was really excited. When we arrived, lots of food was on-hand and tons of beer was stored in lined trash cans filled with ice. That was nutty.

Anyway, Alex Van Halen was drinking a whole pitcher of beer like it was one glass. Man, those guys drank like fishes.

My girlfriend asked me, "Do you really know David Lee Roth?

"Sure, wanna meet him?"

I walked over to David while she was sipping her beer and asked if he would play along with what I had planned in mind. We both walked over to my girlfriend and David asked her,

"Hey, what's your name darlin'? Don'tcha know Ajay and I go way back? He's, my sidekick."

He then kicked me in the ass.

You should have seen the look on her face. She was in shock! It was great. Cool time. Cool fun.

My last story is when I met Joe Walsh. It was when his solo album, *The Confessor*, came out in 1985. He signed a few things for me that day: A Warner Brothers' bio on his career, and the album cover of *Yer Album* from when he played with the James Gang. *The Confessor* was not my favorite album. As a matter of fact, I think it sucked. I talked to him briefly about his previous albums.

"*Yer Album* was the greatest rock album of its time. The James Gang's best," I told him, and I meant it.

He replied, "All right," smiled and left. Really cool laid-back dude. Funny, we didn't even talk about when he played with the Eagles. From Cleveland, Ohio, The James Gang were just as powerful as Cream. Their cover version of "Bluebird" by Buffalo Springfield was brilliant. So was their version of The Yardbirds' "Lost Woman." Back in those days, Joe's guitar work was flawless. Jim Fox, who played drums, was also solid. He joined The James Gang after playing with The Outsiders. They had a huge hit "Time Won't Let Me." Tom Kriss, their bass player, was also fantastic. What a powerhouse of a band.

Well, getting back to that year, 1982, as mentioned earlier, a new format of recorded music was surfacing that would catch the eyes and ears from music enthusiasts around the world: the compact disc. This new format, which was developed by Phillips and Sony, could handle up to eighty minutes of digitally uncompressed audio recorded music. I remember the special meeting about this when the whole warehouse of employees and office were notified.

This new explosion in the field of recorded music raised many eyebrows with questions and concerns. The meeting lasted about an hour with full support and all questions answered. The emotions brought on by the possibility of eliminating vinyl LP's and other formats was interesting. But nevertheless, vinyl kept on selling. Also, since the CD was in its infancy state, not that many titles were being produced. But, by the time I left W.E.A. Corp., a tremendous number of titles were forthcoming.

Looking back on my departure from W.E.A. Corp. around January 1985, at first, I searched in the industry for other record labels to work for, when by chance I noticed a job opening for an import music distributor named Sounds Good. I worked there till the very end upon their closure in June of 1987. I must tell you, in those few years, I learned a lot about the world of imports, including licensing, royalties and more. I was hired as a West Coast Sales Representative, which included traveling to chain stores such as Tower Records, taking inventory, merchandising and sales. I also worked in the office selling prerecorded import and domestic compact discs, vinyl records, cassette and music videotapes, plus imported magazine trades such as *NME, Mojo, Melody Maker, Beatles Monthly* and *Uncut* to specific national accounts in the United States. We also had many exclusives, Chameleon Music Group being an important one. The record label was formed by producer and former Capitol Records A&R executive Stephen Powers in association with Bob Marin, owner of Sounds Good, and co-owner Richard Foos, who was co-founder of Rhino Records. Richard was an interesting character. He talked to me on occasion asking questions and advice regarding compilations that might do well on the Rhino Label. I gave him plenty of ideas and told him I wanted a cut if they were used and they sold well. He just smiled, said, "Thanks," then walked away. Much like working for W.E.A., many recording artists dropped by Sounds Good to say hello.

Susanna Hoffs, from The Bangles, came by with her mother one afternoon. We were distributing *The Allnighter* soundtrack for the movie *The Allnighter*, which her mother, Tamara Simon Hoffs had directed. This was in May of 1987. I walked Susanna around the warehouse. She picked up a few records like Big Star's "*#1 Record* and *Radio City*, which was a two-for-one import. I told her she had good taste. We talked for a while and hung out. Afterwards, she signed a bunch of large movie posters of *The Allnighter* for some of our key accounts that purchased the soundtrack LP. She was cool, and it was nice of her to stop by.

During that same year, our company distributed John Kay and Steppenwolf's *Rock and Roll Rebels* album. It was on a strange label called Qwill. A listening party was held at Yamashiro's Japanese Restaurant, high up in the Hollywood Hills. This restaurant has a long, deep history. The architecture was magnificent. Many hand-carved artifacts surrounding the establishment. In 2012, it was added to the National Register of Historic places, according to the National Park Service. A group of us were situated near the end of the restaurant where you could look out the windows to view the beautiful outdoor Japanese gardens.

John Kay, the lead vocalist, brought his daughter with him. He was a pretty tall dude, over six feet. What a fun night that was with various sushi rolls, hand rolls, shrimp and vegetable tempura, yakitori, nigiri and sashimi, miso soup and Japanese salad being served. The Pagoda Bar lounge was cool, offering exotic cocktails; however, we mostly drank beer and Saki that night. Back then the food was exceptional. Years later, we heard many crazy horror stories about how rancid the food was. But it's still in operation today and known as an Asian Fusion restaurant with a similar vibe.

That night was special. We had other good times at Sounds Good. Every year at Christmas, the owners would hold a company dinner at Twin Dragon Chinese Restaurant located on Pico Boulevard in Los Angeles. It was also Bob Marin's favorite place to dine. It always had a festive atmosphere, and the food was always delicious. It's still open today.

Sounds Good was in Hawthorne, California. An interesting trivial fact is that The Beach Boys went to Hawthorne High School in the 1950's. It was located two blocks away from our office.

Anyway, one of the things that was a bit of a gray area is that, besides vinyl records, we distributed oversized music artist subway posters. I never really knew what vendor we purchased them from. Rock Scene Distributors does ring a bell, but I'm not exactly sure. My first guess was our suppliers in the U.K. The subway posters were made of thick linen and looked awesome. I didn't think they were officially licensed, though, and I was a bit skeptical. That could have been one of the many reasons this cool company fell apart. Many "cease and desist" letters came through the mail during the years I worked there, and they were handled with caution.

Well, sure enough, years later, I read an article in some European art magazine about a graphic artist/photographer named Barney Bubbles who, in September of 1977, designed a series of five posters that measured 60" x 40" for a Stiff Records Package Tour consisting of Elvis Costello, Nick Lowe, Ian Dury,

Wreckless Eric and Larry Wallis. I found out that he was the art director for Stiff Records. Now, that certainly made sense. We stocked these same posters and then some. Even larger posters of concert tours (such as Madonna's). They weren't cheap, either. As it turned out, they were bootleg replicas that looked darn close to the real deal. I purchased an Elvis Costello and Madonna poster. Sad news is, I don't remember whatever happened to them as I moved so many times. Must've lost them in the shuffle, floating around somewhere in La La Land.

Being an avid collector of rock 'n' roll memorabilia since my early teens, this just wasn't a typical thing for me, losing valuables. Maybe they were stolen from my office? Who the hell knows? Well, Sounds Good got in trouble for what they referred to in the music industry as parallel imports. Many imports we stocked from U.K. and Japan had bonus tracks and, in some cases, unreleased tracks that were not included on domestic-released copies. The Ventures are a prime example. Having a massive catalog of over two hundred recordings, many of their releases were Import Only, such as *Live in Japan*, pressed strictly for the Japanese market and not to be distributed in the United States. Surprisingly, Capitol/Liberty Records licensed plenty of their tunes overseas.

Anyway, this can be discussed on many levels, but at that time it was a sin to distribute them in the United States. One afternoon, I was transferred a phone call from Tower Record's main office in Sacramento. I'll never forget that day, as it was one of Tower's executive staff warning me of some import product, they received from Sounds Good that they got busted for. His name was Bob Delanoy. At that time, he was Vice President of Retail Record Sales. He told me, "These vinyl import recordings you sold us will be coming back to you in a large return."

This was a crucial time in the music business before imported product was widely accepted many years later. All sales reps had the knowledge and were careful what territories to sell to— meaning not in high profile areas. Some of these releases we imported from Russia and Italy, for example, were questioned as to who paid the royalties and who licensed the albums. Was the Harry Fox Agency notified? Harry Fox is the nation's leading provider of rights management, licensing and royalty services to the record industry publishers, artists and labels. When Sounds Good closed their doors and shut down, I truly believe Tower Records and a few other larger chain stores and one-stops put them out of business.

Thankfully, some of my established accounts were looking out for me. They mentioned another upcoming importer with killer prices that I needed to phone. Furthermore, they said I would be a big asset to this company as they needed help. That company? Digital Waves Corporation. Their offices were in Costa Mesa, California. I made the initial phone call, then got a response back for an interview. I drove out to meet the owners for that interview. Fuck me, they sure had lots of crazy questions. But I answered them all with pure confidence.

After my interview, we shook hands, and one of the owners showed me their inventory. When I spotted what was in that warehouse, I then knew why they asked me so many freaking questions. I was looking at the most requested Beatles compact discs ever made up to that time period. *Beatles: Ultra Rare Tracks, Volumes 1 and 2*, which were on the Swinging Pig Label, apparently from Japan. (I had read about these just prior to this meeting.) The CD covers were in day glow green and orange. In the December 1988 issue of *Goldmine* magazine, they were written up with a review that shocked and delighted many fans. Every record store in the country was asking for these discs! Believe it or not, Digital Waves was the exclusive distributor with the pair wholesaling at $21.99 per disc. Yes, they were unauthorized recordings. The sound quality was lifted directly from master tapes and clean acetates. As a matter of fact, the sound quality actually outperformed EMI'S official Beatles CD's!

Capitol/EMI was extremely embarrassed about this, as they did not know how in the world these recordings leaked out. Meanwhile, I was called in for a second interview and hired that day, which was a week after my initial visit. I must have passed their scrutiny with flying colors because the owner said, "We're glad to have you on board," and shook my hand. It was June 15th, 1987.

On my first day of work, I phoned up one of my top independent retail stores. They purchased one hundred copies each of The Beatles' *Ultra Tracks*. That sale alone was $4,398, and we hadn't even started my customer's order yet.

At this point, residing in the San Fernando Valley, it would be over an hour's drive to get to work. My mother had just moved to Newport Beach in Orange County, California. She lived in a nice place called Park Newport. They had two beautiful Olympic-sized pools and a large jacuzzi, plus racquetball, handball, tennis and basketball courts! My gosh, they even had their own local market on the premises!

So, I guess you can figure out what happened next. I called her to discuss my plans on furthering my career. At that time, my sister had moved to Los Angeles, as had my brother. I moved my stuff into my mom's condominium. It had two bedrooms and two bathrooms and worked out fine and dandy. It provided plenty of room to store my stuff until I found a new place to live. It was just ten minutes away from my new office. From 1988–2003, I worked for this company that eventually changed its name to Phantom Sound and Vision.

This was the longest job I ever had as well as the craziest, nuttiest, zaniest, fun job ever. They paid high wages and, at times, things got to be very stressful. But we all worked through it. Oh, and what a cast of characters worked for that company! Honestly, could write a whole book about my wild ride with Phantom. However, I'll share with you the best stories.

But before we go through my journey with this company, I'd like to share with you a memorable time I had meeting guitarist Jeff Healey. For those of you who may not heard of him, he was a Canadian blues/rock vocalist, guitarist and songwriter. He was also blind. With that said, a gal I was dating at the time told me her girlfriend was an extra in the film, *Roadhouse*. She invited us to see Jeff Healey, who was playing live at a club in Malibu. It was a closed private event. We drove on Pacific Coast Highway from the San Fernando Valley.

I remember, it was a beautiful summer's night and I had my sunroof open. This was around late 1989, after the movie was done with production. That movie starred Patrick Swayze as a bouncer working in a rough, tough, rowdy bar in the deep South. Actors Sam Elliot, Kelly Lynch and Ben Gazzara also starred in the film but were not at this wrap-up party.

So, after they played, I walked up to Jeff and asked him, "How in the world did you learn how to play guitar on your lap?" It' was so unorthodox, I could not understand. The riffs he played were totally insane and blew me away. I was drinking a beer when talking to him. Then, I don't know why, but I asked him if he could hold his hand up against mine. He smirked and said okay. My God, his hand was huge!

We talked about guitars before his next set. Such a nice guy. As cool as can be. Many years later, I met him again in Dana Point at the Doheny Blues Festival. He was walking on the concert grounds with a wooden cane. I recognized him immediately, then walked over to say hello, and asked him if he remembered me from that time he played in Malibu. He shook my hand and said, "Yes, I remember." My Brother Kenny took a photo of us which I treasure.

Sadly, he passed away from lung cancer at only forty-one years old in 2008. That was a very sad day for me.

Well, back to my days at Phantom. One of my accounts was Beat Music in Modesto, California. The owner, Nick, happened to be good friends with Rick Wakeman (keyboardist) and Jon Anderson (vocalist) from the band Yes. Always wondered why owner Nick purchased so much stuff from me from Yes, Rick Wakeman, and related artists.

One nice summer day in the mid-1990's, Nick called me to say that Rick was in town visiting and asked me if they could swing by to say hello before traveling to Los Angeles. After clearing it with the owners of Phantom, I drove out to meet them in Laguna Beach for a quick bite. Then they followed me back to our offices for a meet-and-greet session with our special guest, Rick Wakeman. I cannot begin to tell you all the silly questions some of the salespeople asked. It didn't seem to bother Rick, who was so wonderful to do this at a moment's notice. He shared many stories that were unexpected and even brought up his wife, who was a close friend of Linda (Eastman) McCartney. (It was the first time any of us heard of Linda's battle with breast cancer which would end her life at the age of fifty-six.)

I thanked Rick for being so gracious signing autographs and hanging out with our entourage. Many employees told me afterwards that that was one of the most magical days they had spent at work and thanked me.

Chapter Five
End of the '80's!
Off to the 1990's and Beyond!

During my years working at Phantom, I had many special moments. In November of 1992, one of the women who worked at the front desk transferred a call that she knew I'd be able to handle. It was from a gentleman who worked for David Letterman on the *Tonight Show*. He was David's talent researcher. He told me that actor Kevin Costner was going to be making a guest appearance soon. He phoned because Kevin played in a band called Roving Boy, and they were going to discuss his life in music on the show. He was told our company carried imported product and wondered if we stocked a CD that Costner's band had released called, *The Simple Truth*.

Sure enough, it was in stock and imported from Japan. He used his credit card to purchase it ahead of time. Just weeks later, I received a package from NBC Entertainment in New York. When I opened the package, I found two t-shirts enclosed with the NBC Logo and a letter that read as follows:

November 20th, 1992
Dear A.J.,
Thanks for your help in getting me the Kevin Costner CD. As you are probably aware, the CD was neither mentioned nor shown during Costner's appearance, which is unfortunate, given the effort we all went through to get this thing. I've enclosed a couple of T-Shirts for all your help.

Thanks again.
Sincerely,
Jay Johnson

Turned out, one tee shirt was small and other was medium. I gave both to the woman at front office who had transferred the call. She was happy.

But one event occurred that I'll treasure for the rest of my life; it happened that same year in 1992. After speaking with our buying department, I phoned Barking Pumpkin Records office in Los Angeles. It was basically, at that time, a mail-order company. Gail Zappa answered the phone. I think she was running the whole show, meaning, taking care of the business aspects while Frank Zappa was on tour. I told her my name and the company I worked for, then explained that we were branching out in distributing a few more independent, domestic labels, and we wanted to see if we could distribute and sell the Barking Pumpkin label to our retail stores. I added that I was a big fan of Frank's music and most everyone I worked with was an audiophile/musicologist. She asked me quite a few questions, then asked for our business address to send a catalog to. At the end of our conversation, I jokingly asked if maybe Frank could sign something for me. "Sure," she said.

Weeks later, I received a catalog with distributor pricing and a whole mess of whacky paraphernalia. When I opened this package, a photo slipped out on the floor. I couldn't believe my eyes! It was a glossy color photo of Frank Zappa, autographed, "To Andy, FZ," and dated "1992" in black marker. It's been hanging up in my office ever since.

Another unusual story happened years later in 1998. One of my accounts told me about this crazy psychedelic pop recording Andrew Gold made in his home studio. I investigated, which led me to getting in touch with Andrew Gold on the phone. You may remember his big hit, "Lonely Boy," from 1977. We talked a bit about music and what this recording was all about and what it meant to him. He explained everything in detail, and I was totally psyched.

What a wonderful conversation we had! Real cool guy—cooler than I thought he'd be. He sent me a promo copy to give to my buyer. After listening, my buyer decided to bring in fifty copies of this CD to start off with, then reorder when sold out. It was reordered for another 50 copies, but unfortunately, it was never to be seen again after that.

My personal thoughts on his idea and recording were pure bliss. A true masterpiece. He called it *Fraternal Order of The All - Greetings from Planet Love* on J-Bird Records (CD only format). To me, this recording was impeccable. You could hear shades of The Beach Boys, The Byrds, Dylan, The Beatles, The Doors, Tom Petty and lots more inflections from that time period in the late 60's. It was something Andrew had dreamed about and followed through with. If you can find it on the internet or record stores around the states, I highly recommend you get yourself a copy. It truly was the record Andrew had always wanted to do back in 1967/1968 era. You could swear it was recorded back in the day as it was so accurately produced!

Sadly, years later I learned that in June of 2011, he died at age fifty-nine from some fucked up cancer. I miss him and think about him when I play that recording from time to time.

Well, as I mentioned, there were plenty of nutty people that worked at Phantom. One character from our sales office came up to me one afternoon and asked for a favor, as he knew I was a collector of rock 'n' roll memorabilia. It turned out that his next-door neighbor had been dating Mitch Mitchell, the original drummer from the Jimi Hendrix Experience. She hadn't seen him in over a year and asked my buddy Clyde if he knew anyone that could sell Mitch's belongings that he'd left in her shed, located behind her house. So, I met Clyde at the woman's home in Costa Mesa to see for myself and determine all the contents' value. When we both walked in her backyard towards the shed, I noticed a black bass drum traveling case outside. It was empty. He then opened the lock to the shed with a key and in we went. It was awfully hot that day and worse inside of this shed, which was filled with spiderwebs hanging down, a few touching my face.

I yelled at my friend, "What the hell, Clyde! This place is a mess!"

I tripped over a few things, then to my right I spotted two vintage stacks of acoustic amplifiers with two guitar cases on the floor. My heart started to race as I thought they may have belonged to Hendrix. Well, I opened both cases to check, but the guitars were both for right-handed players. So, I figured Mitch probably dabbled around and played just for fun. One was a Fender Telecaster, the other a Gibson Les Paul. They weren't rare or collectible, but those acoustic amplifiers were definitely valuable and in great shape. As I continued looking, I noticed a stack of records. I looked through them all. Once again, nothing worthy, unless you loved Dean Martin. The genre of music in that stack of records, couldn't have reflected Mitch's taste. But who knows?

That's when I started to doubt that this was the real deal—until I found a briefcase sitting on top of an old wooden desk. My heart started to race again in the anticipation of what might be stored inside. When opening this suitcase, to my surprise, I discovered inside a whole load of letters addressed to Mitch Mitchell from Al Hendrix, Jimi's Father. I also found a few from Noel Redding, the original bass player from Hendrix Experience. I yelled, "Praise Jesus!"

Clyde started cracking up. He hadn't seen any of this stuff beforehand. This felt like Indiana Jones searching for the Lost Ark. While sorting through this case, I also found an 8" x 10" B&W glossy photo of Stevie Ray Vaughn, signed to Mitch. This suitcase was a *Goldmine*!

I continued walking through to the back of the shed and spotted two drum kits! Both were Ludwig. One set was silver sparkled (from what I can remember). The other one I can't recall, however, there were a whole bunch of cymbals laying around with a bunch of drumsticks. Stamped on those drumsticks was the label "Simon Phillips Pro Mark Hickory."

When we left, we were sweating like crazy. I told Clyde I'd come back with my camera and take photos, then present them to the appropriate auction houses such as Bonham's Auction House, Butterfield and Butterfield, Sotheby's and Heritage Auctions. The results? They were *All* interested. But the following week, after all I went through, the woman—an unstable nutcase—had decided to back out because she got scared. I guess her behavior didn't surprise me, as Mitch played in Hollywood with a lot of notable musicians; sometimes they played gigs at The Coconut Teaser on the Sunset Strip. So, in good faith Clyde told me, "Hey, I have something for you." He then handed me a pair of Mitch Mitchell's drumsticks. They're now stored in my box of rock 'n' roll treasures.

Sadly, Mitch passed away in his sleep on November 12th, 2008 in Portland, Oregon, while on The Experience Hendrix Tour. He was only sixty-two.

Around this same time in 1989, one of the owners of Phantom Imports wrote me a check for $14,000 for me to purchase my first home. It was a nice, spacious condo with two bedrooms and two baths, with a back deck and enclosed two-car garage. He also set me up with a real estate agent with whom he had worked with on many occasions and enjoyed a friendship with.

My new pad was located in Newport Beach, California. I actually paid him back within that same year! This I must praise him for, as no other owner of any company for whom I have worked for ever did such a thing for me.

In the 1990's, the company was doing well. I got one of my good friends with whom I'd worked with at Sounds Good, the opportunity joining our other buyer to help grow this company even further. Sometimes our suppliers would provide concert tickets to various shows. Just before my birthday on July 23rd 1992, my buyer, Peter, received two complimentary tickets to see The Charlie Watts Quintet at The Palace in Hollywood, with reserved seats and dinner provided. The Palace was located on 1735 N. Vine Street and still exists to this day, but in 2002, the name changed to The Avalon Ballroom. A rich history exists about this theatre, but I'll leave it at that.

I drove the two of us that evening, leaving from Orange County, which was about an hour's drive in traffic. While we were having a drink at the bar, I bumped into Ian McLagan, the keyboardist for the band Small Faces. He recognized me from my old band days with Killer Kane. Since he was English, I naturally introduced him to my buyer, Peter, who was also from the U.K. We all shared a pint of beer together.

The evening got even better as Ian said to us, "C'mon, Chaps, we're going to meet Charlie."

Peter looked at me like, "How the fuck do you know Ian?"

Anyway, he was delighted. We walked through the corridor to the backstage area and met all the members of the band after one spectacular show. We had a lovely time with even more food and more alcohol!

When I spoke with Charlie Watts, I couldn't understand what the heck he was saying, as he had this heavy east-end Cockney accent. Peter followed him and completely understood every word. Charlie then signed my concert ticket in pencil. I could hardly read it, but who cares?

When driving home, Peter told me he couldn't have had more fun. What a night that was!

This company had many seasonal parties. One of the owners just loved celebrating Halloween. Every other year, he would invite employees to his family home for a company Halloween party. One year, my brother and I dressed up as Bevis and Butthead. They were a big deal at the time and featured on MTV. Everyone laughed their asses off. The eyeholes in the masks were hard to see through, but there was a small opening in the mouth so we could breathe and drink beer. People took many photos of us because we really played the part.

I got terribly drunk. When walking in the backyard, my brother yelled, "Look Out!" It was too late; I walked right into a pond and got soaking wet. Of course, that was a funny sight, I guess, as onlookers saw the whole thing take place. right before their very eyes. They told me it was the greatest thing they've ever seen, especially wearing that ridiculous costume. It completely fit the character. Luckily, my boss had an extra pair of shorts and a t-shirt for me to wear. My sneakers were soaking wet, so he found a pair of thongs for me to wear. He then laughed and said, "You're a mess!"

What a night that was. Once a year we'd have an annual Christmas party. Sometimes it was held at a hotel, sometimes at a restaurant. But one particular party took place aboard a massive yacht the owners of the company rented out for the night. It launched from the docks of Newport Beach on Christmas 2001. This party got way out of control in more ways than you could imagine. For instance, the Coast Guard gave many warnings to the captain of this yacht.

I remember one fellow from our warehouse crew was completely drunk off his ass. and as he was trying to walk down the spiral walkway, he lost his balance and grabbed his brother for help; but as it turned out, they both fell off the railway right into the ocean. There were fights between boyfriends and girlfriends. Major drinking was on both decks of the yacht. People were yelling and screaming and cussing at other boats nearby. Locked doors hid the sexual activity, and a whole bunch of pot smokers on the high deck, thought they were on Top of the world. It was like a low-budget B-movie coming to life. I'd call it *Mondo Turbo Sexo Destroyo*.

This company even had their own limousine! I drove it home one night when our limo driver at the time couldn't handle his liquor. We'd participated in an event at the Marriott Hotel, it was a NARM Convention (National Association of Recording Merchandisers). The driver threw his guts out and was fired that same evening. It was fun driving that limousine. After dropping off two people, I drove home, but I couldn't turn too well. Still, I made it back in one piece. The owner called me and said, "Just park the limo in your guest parking lot across from your condo, and I'll get someone to take it back in the morning."

During those years, I was so thankful I had the funds to purchase the high-end audio and video equipment I'd always dreamed of: a five-channel amplifier; a preamplifier; loud-speakers; a turntable; a Blu-ray player; all-code DVD player; a Laserdisc player; plus, my first generation 34" HD Hi-Scan 1080i monitor. You could unbelievably watch two TV programs at the same time. It even had a built-in sound system with a sub-woofer. Sony was one of the first companies to produce such an amazing HD widescreen television in 1998. I just had to have this set!

At that time, my friends had just heard about what this new HD talk was all about. Fourteen years later, when it blew out, it took two big dudes to pull it away into the dumpster.

Each family was allowed a few large items to get recycled per year from where I lived. When first visiting this retail store (Ken Crane's) to purchase it, I was struck in awe at the most crystal-clear, extra-sharp picture I'd ever seen—even to this day! Because this was not an LCD/LED plasma set, but one with built-in picture tubes, the difference was tremendous. I remember, it took three people to pick up and deliver it to my condo in Newport Beach. It was a heavy-duty monster of a set that weighed 205 pounds. I purchased it for a whopping $4,500! After fourteen years, guess I got my money's worth, so I really shouldn't complain. What an experience!

During this time, my music collection was growing so rapidly with domestic and imported compact discs, DVD's and vinyl LP's, I had two custom cabinets designed and built out of pine and painted in turquoise with glass inserted in both doors to view collection. Cabinets could store up to one thousand pieces of vinyl each. My place was beginning to look like a fully packed record store!

As you can see by now, music is my life. Lived it, breathed it, and played it!

While living in Newport Beach, I had many movie-night get-togethers. Friends would bring over appetizers and drinks, from wine to beer to hard liquor. My next-door neighbor never complained about my loud music. She was a stripper, so she really wasn't home from early evening to real late at night. A few times, things got so loud that neighbors across the street, on the corner lot from my end unit, complained to the cops. Yes, the police dropped by many times and warned me to cease all music and movies by 10:00 p.m., or I'd get fined.

One weekend night, about 6:00 p.m. when I was having dinner, I heard a loud thump from next door. I knocked on their front door and it swung open. To my surprise, lying on the kitchen floor, practically unconscious, was that blonde stripper I mentioned before. Her name was Sunny (I don't think that was her real name). So, I'm thinking to myself, *what do I do now?*

I saw an empty bottle of Jägermeister on the floor beside her. I tried to wake her up, then I felt her pulse. She mumbled a bunch of gibberish that made no sense at all. I must admit, in just a pink bra and faded, ripped up denim shorts, she looked really hot! Well, I knew the right thing to do. I picked her up, placed her on her bed, then closed the door and left. Days later, she knocked on my door and thanked me for helping her. Then I asked her, "Honestly, do you remember drinking that nasty Jägermeister left on the floor?"

She just smiled. We got to be friends, till she got evicted. Most likely it was because of her boyfriend, who seemed shady, most likely a drug dealer. The police came by many times. They never did get the real story.

Other than that, I loved living so close to the beach. I rode my mountain bike along different trails and took long journeys from Newport Beach to Seal Beach on the coast; I also rode to Laguna Beach in the opposite direction. Obviously, I took a break here and there to jump in the ocean to cool off.

I stayed quite active during my ten years residing at my Newport Beach condo. One Saturday morning I rode to the Stuft Surfer for breakfast on the strip. I was friends with Bob, the owner. Believe it or not, he was also a pharmacist. He enjoyed music and had ordered a CD from me which I brought over that morning. Baseball player Reggie Jackson was there having break-fast too and asked who I was to Bob. Bob said, "Ajay's my music guy. He used to play in a band!"

Reggie was probably wondering who I was and I'm guessing

he was also wondering if I knew who he was.

When leaving, I said "Hey, Reggie, what's up?"

You should have seen the look on his face. He looked puzzled; it was hilarious.

At another time in 1999, my friend called me on my cell phone while I was having lunch near the Newport Pier. He told me he just read an article in the local newspaper that there was going to be a private show at Muldoons's Irish Pub, located in Fashion Island/Newport Beach.

"Who's playing?" I asked him.

"Ray Manzarek, the keyboardist from The Doors, is going to perform a private, free, unannounced show, but you have to get there quick as place could get crowded."

"No way!" I yelled.

I rode my bike as fast as I could, sweating my ass off. I only had a $5 bill in my pocket and no wallet or ID. I figured I'd purchase one beer. When I arrived, the pub was packed. I locked up my bicycle outside and luckily found a seat. It was the most intimate, unreal show. Just Ray and his keyboards on a tiny little stage performing many songs from The Doors. When he sang, trying to replicate Jim Morrison's voice, on "Riders on the Storm," it was unbelievable—mesmerizing and kind of spooky. It was as if Jim Morrison was trying to channel through Ray spiritually. It really freaked me out.

The lucky patrons witnessing this hour-plus show were also fixated. His musical performance, along with telling stories about his years playing in The Doors, was fascinating. After he finished playing, people came up to talk to him and ask for autographs. When finally meeting him, I shook his hand and thanked him for the most entertaining time I'd had in a long while.

"Thanks," he told me, then added with a smile, "Dig yourself, dig deep." Very spiritual, down-to-earth musician. Never have I forgotten that moment. While writing about this event, I contacted Muldoon's directly to find out more such as the exact date he performed. Their manager told me on their Guinness Wall of Fame, they have a plaque hanging at the pub that states April 18th, 1999. He then told me how amazing it was that I had been at that show and thanked me for the phone call. In tribute, Ray Manzarek passed away on May 20th, 2013. He was seventy-four years old.

Well, I've gotta say, many special events occurred in Newport Beach and surrounding areas, and I was lucky to have been there to celebrate. Another day I won't forget happened to be on my birthday. July 25th 1997. I had to RSVP in advance since this was a much-anticipated event. I was invited to the Fingerhut Gallery in Laguna Beach to the premier exhibition of renowned artist Peter Max. Since my mother loved his work, I brought her with me to view his new paintings, drawings and sculptures. After all, she was the one who opened my eyes to his fine art in the first place.

Before heading out, I grabbed my old pamphlet from his art exhibition in New York that I'd saved all those years. I remember my mother bringing me with her that day, back in 1969, when I was only fifteen years old. When meeting Peter, towards the end of show, I introduced myself and my mother to him. We shook hands, then I showed him the original pamphlet I'd brought with me.

Right at that moment, he smiled and said, "Wow, do you know that was my very first show in New York?" He signed the front cover: "Mr. A.J. Love, Max 97." As I'm writing this, Peter is in his eighties, but sadly suffers from advanced dementia. He hasn't painted seriously in years. In recent articles, his friends state he doesn't know what year it is, and spends most afternoons relaxing on his lounge chair in his apartment, looking out at the Hudson River.

After my mother died, I found a whole bunch of Peter Max collectibles: a ceramic ashtray; printed pillowcases and bed sheets; plus, several silicone-rubber dinner placemats. Boy, I wish I had his original artwork. These few things, however, make me happy.

Another event I attended was on April 24th 1999. It was a rainy Saturday evening from 6:00-9:00 p.m., I was at The Sutton

Place Art Gallery in the Sutton Place Hotel on MacArthur Blvd. I had received in the mail an invitation for the opening reception of the photography of Henry Diltz . . . a collection of his rock 'n' roll album cover art and photographs. It was RSVP only, as space was limited. Knowing about Henry's work beforehand, I pretty much knew what to expect. I figured I'd better dress appropriately.

Upon arrival, delicious hors d'oeuvres and fine wine were served. Walking through the gallery, I was amazed to see a few legendary album covers, such as The Doors *Morrison Hotel* and Crosby, Stills, Nash and Young's debut album printed in 20" x 16" x 30" editions that were for sale. Met Graham Nash while we were drinking wine. He was so cool to talk to, mentioning the times when Henry took photos of CSNY through the years. Many celebrities were present that night from movies, music and television; I supposed they were there in support of Henry's works. Fifty framed, limited prints were up for sale and hung on the walls of the gallery covering the era from the band America to Frank Zappa. They were also selling a CD ROM, *Under the Covers,* of most all of Henry Diltz's work, with interactions. What I was primarily interested in was the *Jimi Hendrix at Woodstock* from 1969 that I spotted across the room. Jimi was my all-time hero of guitar players growing up and to this very day!

I had to talk with Henry about that iconic photo. We did talk for a while about his early days playing banjo and clarinet with the Modern Folk Quartet, and how he got to be one of the most recognized rock 'n' roll photographers known today. What's crazy was he just took photos of his friends for fun back in the '60's. Those friends happened to be The Lovin' Spoonful; Crosby, Stills and Nash; Mama Cass Elliot of The Mamas and the Papas; and Joni Mitchell. It was an interesting time in California, the 1960's. Like the Summer of Love phenomenon in 1967. When asking Henry about that Jimi photo, he told me only a few official staff photographers were allowed backstage at Woodstock and Monterey Pop.

"When I took the photo," he said, "it was early in the morning just before sunrise. A field of mud was on the grounds with a whole batch of surviving concertgoers still hanging out. Thousands of people had already left by the time Jimi started playing."

The way he told his story, I could picture myself there. I hung on his every word.

"When Jimi started playing 'The Star-Spangled Banner,'" he continued, "that's when this famous photo was shot."

Only 275 prints were produced worldwide. Yep, I had to purchase it. I snagged #104 of 275. I had to wait after the show was over to pick up my framed photo. At about $600, I have no regrets. It has escalated in value ever since. After all, I've been collecting rock 'n' roll memorabilia from an early age, and from the looks of it, I don't think it will end till I'm gone from this earth.

♪♫♪

So, around this time it came to a point for me to move on. Once the association dues went up where I lived in Newport Beach, I knew it was time. We're talking about an increase of an additional $200 a month! Many condominium homeowners complained about that as well; I wasn't the only one. Many meetings were held regarding this issue at the community office located right up the street. But that wasn't all that was going on.

Word spread quickly that there was a pedophile living in the neighborhood. Every homeowner was in shock. Many families had children and they protested outside the condo where this person was staying. This story was even broadcast on television and the local newspaper. Many residents put their condos up for sale. It was kind of ridiculous but serious at the same time. Forty homes were eventually up for sale as nothing was immediately done about this situation. It took a while to fix too! The Homeowners Association received tons of phone calls, many of them threatening! They were worried.

Seeking another place to live after my ten years' stay was challenging. I chose a local real estate agent in town. She showed me beachfront places along Huntington Beach, Corona Del Mar, Laguna Beach and Dana Point. After looking at more than twenty homes and getting completely frustrated, I finally found a wonderful home located in a cul-de-sac overlooking the mountains and the ocean in Dana Point. It had three bedrooms, two bathrooms and a large back deck, plus an oversized pool. Outside on that back deck where the pool was located, I said to my agent, "This is a *Million-dollar view!*"

It wasn't cheap, but I had a steady income. I submitted my offer on Christmas Day 2002. Early that evening, my offer was accepted. On January 21st 2003, I moved in. This was the first real house I had ever owned, and it was a bit overwhelming at first.

But I got accustomed quickly. I rented out two bedrooms to good friends, one female and one male with a dog. Things worked out well. We had many outdoor pool parties, Tiki cocktails—the works!

Again, like when we moved from New York to Michigan, I was happy not having anyone living above or below me. I just had two neighbors who thankfully never complained. One was a piano teacher. The other was a retired swinger—he was some character! He had two cars: a classic 1960's Corvette, and a Cadillac, plus a large yacht that he stored at the Dana Point Harbor.

Every year, my local community held a Fourth of July Parade that started right in front of my house, practically on my driveway! I couldn't believe it.

My neighbors asked me, "Didn't the people that sold you the house tell you?"

Well, that first year, right outside my front door, I heard a whole bunch of noise that woke me. The mayor of Dana Point came by on a large, beautifully decorated float leading the parade up the hill. A flock of people were outside on other floats with dogs, cats, and little kids. Every year at my home you could see fireworks from three or four different directions, right from my back deck: Dana Point Harbor, San Juan Capistrano, San Clemente Beach and Mission Viejo.

This home was quite magical. Feng Shui in every way. At one point, I had close to twenty friends swimming in my pool, it was that freaking big! It took a lot of water to fill up that damn pool. My water bills were exorbitantly high. One afternoon, just for kicks, my crazy friend Kevin dove in the deep end to measure the depth of pool. Results were thirteen feet deep. Swan Pools was the manufacturer. They started their Company in 1954 and are one of the oldest companies still in business. Little did anyone know, back in 1962 when my pool was built, there would be a major water shortage in Southern California just decades later. They don't make pools like that anymore, that's for sure.

Nine months later, on October 2nd 2003, each employee of Phantom Sound and Vision received a letter stating that at 5:00 p.m. that day, they would be relieved of any and all duties as employees of the company. Basically, the company had been *Sold!* No severance pay. No pension. Everyone who worked at the company—including me, of course—was completely devastated. We did have an offer, though, to start work with another distributor, whom I shall leave nameless, as there was a massive lawsuit involved. Years later, on February 13th 2007, a judge dismissed that lawsuit based upon a settlement between both companies. Luckily for me, I had plenty of contacts to choose from when all this took place.

♪♫♪

Well, truth be told, I and a few other salespeople were not happy and chose another company where we felt more comfortable. My new office was on the second floor of an old building in downtown San Clemente, California. Looking out my office window, I could see the ocean. The drive on Pacific Coast Highway every day on my way to work was beautiful. I often thought, this is just too good to be true, while drinking my mint chocolate coffee espresso.

For those next few years, as much fun as I had, it was tense and unpredictable. But, regardless, so many cool things were happening. A late summer event was held for many years called A Taste of Newport. Many local restaurants participated, and live entertainment was featured as well. At the entry gate you would simply purchase a roll of tickets for food-tasting samples and alcoholic drinks. If you ran out, you could always purchase more. Then you'd get handed a wrist band for drinks.

Some years were better than others regarding the entertainment. In September of 2004, I phoned my buyer, Steve, and asked him if he would like to drive out to visit me and go to this event. The Beach Boys were performing, as well as the band Ambrosia. So, he drove out from Redondo Beach and we purchased about twenty dollars' worth of food and drink tickets that we thought would cover us for the day. For some odd reason, I brought my empty CD jewel case of Bruce and Terry in hopes that Bruce Johnston would sign it for me after show. Steve must have been my good luck charm because when we sat down to eat, I found on the ground a whole roll of unused tickets! To be courteous, I asked the fellow near me if he'd dropped them by accident. He said, "Thanks, but no, they're not mine."

When looking at this roll of tickets closely, it was like sixty to seventy dollars' worth of food and drinks. Steve couldn't stop laughing, as he couldn't believe what had just happened. So, we were totally set for food and drinks for the remainder of that late afternoon/early evening. When the Beach Boys took a break, I casually walked over to Bruce alongside of the stage and asked him if he would be kind enough to sign my CD cover of Bruce and Terry.

"Those fuckers at Del Fi! They Screwed me out of a lot of money," he said. Then he noticed the label was Sundazed.

"Okay," he added. "I'll sign this, but make sure that guy behind you signs as well!"

I asked, "Who's that?"

He said, "Terry!"

When I looked behind me, sure enough, once in a million years this could happen: Terry Melcher was standing right behind me with his wife. My God! Being Doris Day's son, Terry fell right into the music scene at an early age, and what a life he'd had. I read all about the true story years ago in the '60's, when the Charles Manson "family" went to the house Sharon Tate lived in. It was Terry Melcher they were looking for! Manson had sent Terry Melcher a demo tape of his music, in an attempt to get a record deal; he felt Terry had given him the brush-off. A few known facts have now surfaced following Doris Day's passing at the age of ninety-seven in May 2019. She may have really saved her only son's life. She told him to move out of that rental property on Benedict Canyon and to move to her home. They shared a close relationship, but besides that, she knew of the goings-on with the Manson family and had a very keen sense. Terry and I talked for a short bit, but No way, would I go there to that horrible time.

Terry asked what line of work I was in. I told him and he asked, "Think you could find my first two solo albums on import CD from Japan? I've been trying for a while."

"We had one of them in stock," I said, "and I could special order the other, no problem."

He gave me his phone number.

"Just call me when it comes in."

I told him I'd purchase it as a favor. He signed my CD, then I shook his hand and told him and his wife that it was nice meeting them both.

As time slipped by, I got so busy that I almost completely forgot my promise. It took a while to get this other CD. It was out of stock from our supplier at the time. It was now late November, two months after we first met, and both CDs were ready to ship out.

When I called Terry, his wife answered. She asked who was calling. I told her, "I'm that guy you met a little while back at the Taste of Newport. I have both those CD's Terry was looking for."

She paused, then said, "Yes, I remember you." She paused again, and then she told me that Terry had passed away.

My heart dropped. I couldn't move; I was in such shock. On November 19th 2004, Terry died at age sixty-two after a long battle with melanoma.

I wished to God; If Only I'd have reached him sooner. I could not have predicted such a thing would happen. That was a sad day for me.

♪♪♪

So, back to me and my comrades from work. We were unsure what the future would hold for us in this business. For one thing, many independent record stores around this time had closed, and to make things more dramatic, from 2006–2007, both Tower Records and Virgin Records had closed all their stores, liquidated and gone bankrupt. If I only had the insight or could have foreseen where this was all going beforehand, then I could have been more prepared. So, check this out: the company where I worked was acquired by the same fucking company who sued them in the first place!

On Wednesday, September 5th 2007, early afternoon, all computers in our office were shut down just as the sole owner's conference phone call ended. I was in shock and felt it was the end of the world for all music retailers and chain stores. The very next day, in *Billboard* magazine's September 6th 2007, issue, it was stated that the terms of the deal were not disclosed. It also stated it was believed that our company moved $40 million a year in volume, and then said the deal was evaluating whether or not to close our warehouse and move inventory to its headquarters. Stories were escalating that more and more independent record stores across the states were closing their doors like a contagious disease. It was getting crazy and times were troubling. Between Napster, Free Downloads, MP3, and streaming such as Pandora, Spotify, iTunes and the digital music revolution, technology was moving quicker than the artists could keep up with. Furthermore, there are more ways now to promote music, thanks to social media platforms like Facebook, Twitter, Instagram and Snapchat.

With all this going on, bet you're wondering if I ever got to play in another band? Well, the answer is no. Not exactly. I did, however, play background acoustic slide guitar throughout the low-budget movie, *Zombie Farm*. It had a cult following when it was released in 2007. The background music was designed like that of a spaghetti western. Believe it or not, many scenes were

shot right at my home in Dana Point and around my neighborhood. Some of the actors fucked my place up a bit, broke a lounge
chair and made a huge mess. I wish I'd known what I was getting
myself into. One scene was shot on my front lawn with a zombie's
"brain" dropping into my pond. It was full of red dye. Am glad I
had no goldfish swimming around at the time.

Other scenes were shot at my next-door neighbors' homes.
They obliged, thinking this was going to be a popular film, especially for teenagers. If they only knew what a low budget film it
really was, they may have backed out. I was a fucking idiot not
charging a fee for full use of my home. I only did it because my
best friend was working on the soundtrack music and was part
of the film crew. The streets were blocked off and the filming
went on for a couple of days. So, just as I imagined, it did fair at
the box office. Many reviews said the same thing: "Don't expect
anything great, just a lot of gore and fun." I think it got 5 out of a
10 on the ratings scale. Not bad, I guess. Could have been worse.

In August of 2008, I found an interesting job on Craigslist
selling and promoting wine, which I'd never done before.
Cameron Hughes founded the company in 2001. His goal was
to offer great wines at affordable prices. You could call him a
modern-day Wine Négociant. I worked for him until 2010.
Interestingly, sometime in 2008, I met Mick Fleetwood at a special wine event featuring his private cellar wines collection. And
I definitely brought with me a few album covers of Fleetwood
Mac to have him sign and, of course, picked up a few bottles of
his Reserve Chardonnay and his Cabernet.

So, here's my story. When I showed him the album cover of
"English Rose," he laughed.

"You know who that bloke is, don't cha?" Before I could say
anything, he said, "That's me in drag!"

Then he told me the whole story how that album cover came
about. We chatted about the old Fleetwood Mac personnel,
before Stevie Nicks, Christine McVie, Lindsey Buckingham and
Bob Welch joined. In my opinion, British blues at its finest.

I could tell Mick really missed those days. He was reminiscing about his old bandmates such as Peter Green. We both agreed he played some memorable guitar breaks and had a very distinguishable, bluesy voice. What a lineup of musicians: Jeremy Spencer, Danny Kirwan, John McVie and of course, Peter Green. It was awesome to meet him, and we had a bit of fun as well.

In 2009, because of my music background, Cameron Hughes chose me to represent the company at MUSEXPO. This was a special event in Los Angeles with about 650 to 1500 attendees from music, television and film. Industry executives and recording artists from around the world attend each year. Cameron Hughes was one of four wineries sponsoring this event. It was held at the London West Hotel, smack in the middle of Hollywood, right off Sunset Boulevard. I have to say, it was exciting pouring wine on the rooftop of the hotel overlooking the whole city. What a spectacular view! There was a pool on the side of this rooftop with a few hot girls swimming. That was equally exciting.

Anyway, this wine-tasting and cocktail reception also offered exotic appetizers and, within one hour, the place was packed. After a while, I asked my partner for a break and, in return, I would bring some food back for both of us. As I was walking through, I bumped into Seymour Stein. I recognized him right away. He was the founder and president of Sire Records. Just by coincidence, he was sampling one of our wines and seemed to be enjoying it. We got to talk about the music scene in New York in the 70's and the bands he had signed through the years. It was so cool meeting him. Upon leaving, he told me that our merlot was his favorite out of all the wines he had tasted that night.

"There are two wines from our company waiting for you at your hotel room. That Merlot is one of them," I assured him. He smiled and thanked me. Afterwards, my partner Paul and I were invited to the Whiskey a Go Go and The Viper Room to see two new independent bands, Purple Melon and Dead Letter Circus.

I thought that night would never end. After the drinking and partying were done, Paul said, "Let's go out to eat!"

He had a company credit card and worked in the San Francisco office with Cameron, so that was nice. After our meal, it was time to head back home. I took a lot of photos at all the events. What a night that was!

So, I still worked part-time for one more music company while selling wine. They distributed Rhino handmade product and many domestic indie labels including their own Collector's Choice-plus import product as well. I sold to my already established accounts while lounging by the pool. Once again, I found myself thinking, *This is the life.* But, as they say, all good things must come to an end.

I didn't want to believe it, but it happened again. This company sold out to that same distributor as mentioned above. This was truly the day the music died. "American Pie," the song by Don McLean, was playing in my head nonstop. This was now the third consecutive company selling out to this distributor, whose name I'll leave blank again to avoid a lawsuit.

I continued working in the wine business and eventually landed a full-time job for one of the better-known wine importers. All this time I did everything I could to keep my home. I rented out two rooms to two women. Things worked out until they fought for use of the bathroom they had to share. Fuck me, I hadn't thought that one out too well. Honestly, at times I felt like Hugh Hefner, considering what went on.

With the help of my friend's landscaping crew, I placed thick bamboo all around my back deck, so it resembled a Hawaiian resort with a Tiki god in my planter and two Tiki torches on each side. I was making decent money again. How I wished I'd found this type of work earlier, as this business seemed to be recession proof—when people are happy, they drink, in celebration they drink, and when depressed, they may drink. The parties continued for a while, music flowed throughout my house and everyone had fun. But, as I'm sure you all recall, the housing bubble crisis hit.

What came next was a dark period for me. Just when I thought things were going smoothly, housing prices began to decline. Driven by supply and demand, this affected many families in the United States, including me. Unfortunately, I didn't understand. When demand decreases, supply increases, resulting in a fall in prices. Even though I still worked, my bills were piling up. With my mortgage and taxes for example, I felt like things were tumbling down for me.

Sure enough, in February of 2012, after exhausting all my finances, I had no choice but to put my home up for short sale. I hired a top-notch bankruptcy attorney and went to court. The results? I figured if I lost my home, I'd most likely have to file for bankruptcy. Well, that's exactly what happened. I was devastated. Never in my life did I ever anticipate this chain of events hitting me in the face. Stories abounded in the news of people committing suicide over this very thing. When leaving court, my attorney said it best: "Look, you've given it your all and lived well. Don't look back, as you'll drive yourself crazy. Just move on. You'll find another place and be okay. I promise. I have many clients that are worse off than you. Many have children. You'll be okay. Build your credit up slowly. Apply for a gas card or a secured credit card." He then shook my hand and said, "You're free."

Well, life was not that simple afterwards. When I thought things couldn't get any worse, on December 31st 2013, my job working for that import wine distributor came to an end. All the things that went on in my head, made me think, *It's the beginning of the end of the world all over again!'*

At that very moment I was lost and worried. Dozens of employees were also let go. Oddly, the next day I received an unexpected phone call from the vice president of the company offering me my job back—but there was a catch: No insurance, no benefits, but double the pay as an independent contractor. He told me he was sorry for what had happened and that the company was going through a transition. He also told me my sales were above most every sales rep and nothing I had done was wrong. They were just downsizing. I didn't want to apply for unemployment, so a few days later, I accepted his offer. The job lasted about seven months.

When it was over, I sent out my resumé to many wine and

spirits companies. At that time, I demoed at Costco locations in Orange County. One weekend when at the San Juan Capistrano location, an older gentleman came up to me and asked what winery I was representing. When I looked at him, I said, "This is crazy, sir, but ya know you look exactly like actor Bert Lahr. But that can't be!"

He smiled and told me, "I'm his son."

He was living with his wife in San Clemente, California. We talked for a short while about the Wizard of Oz movie where his father had played the Cowardly Lion. He told me his dad told him some crazy stories back when he was a kid about the Munchkins and how they were mistreated. He then introduced himself as John Lahr and told me he was a writer. He was a very nice gentleman. I'm glad that I got the chance to meet him.

I continued seeking work, but found out that many jobs turned out to be 1099 independent contractor positions. That seemed odd to me. Apparently, these companies didn't want to pay for insurance benefits. Well, I landed a job for a company in Napa Valley as their Southern California rep. I moved out of Dana Point and rented a room from one of my best friends, who had a large home and two dogs. It was in San Juan Capistrano, across the street from the Sacred Mission. This was a big change for me as I had owned property for so many years. Life was okay without listening to my music in the format I was accustomed to. So, with just my little stereo computer speakers and a subwoofer, I got by and satisfied my needs.

I got used to renting again and led the same life, but I often wondered where I'd be living in the near future. So, I worked two part-time jobs. One was working directly with an owner and winemaker from Paso Robles, California. He needed a salesman to sell his wine and work special events with him. He produced small lots of many wine varietals such as Cabernet Sauvignon, Petite Sirah, Primitivo, Sangiovese and Merlot—less than a thousand cases per year. It was a challenge, selling to specialized markets and restaurants. After a while, it got up to a point, with only getting paid commission, I just couldn't swing that gig any longer. So, I had no choice but to leave . . . but on good terms.

The owner hugged me and said, "Don't be a stranger. I understand."

Times were tough for me, but I never gave up. It seemed that times were also tough for many of the companies where I conducted wine tastings. Fresh and Easy Neighborhood Markets and Haggen Grocery Stores went out of business. This was around 2014–2015 when they filed for bankruptcy. Crazier than that, Cameron Hughes, with whom I started out in the wine world, was bought out in 2017 as part of a bankruptcy court settlement.

At that same time, my mother was also struggling financially. Thankfully, I was able to help her. She was living alone, as her long-time partner moved to an assisted living facility nearby. Unfortunately, he couldn't walk up the stairs to her condo any longer, even with the use of a cane or walker.

She was depressed, living alone. She was eighty-eight years old at that time. My brother and sister contacted me by phone, asking me to help talk her into selling her condo and placing her in the same assisted living residency as her boyfriend. My sister took a plane ride out to finalize things. After we both visited many nursing centers, we agreed it was best for my mother to stay where she felt most comfortable, and that was at her condo. After many discussions, arguing and trying to justify what was "right," on September 30th 2014, I moved into her condo. From that time on, I was a caregiver for my mother. I hadn't exactly planned on that beforehand, but I knew it was seriously the right thing to do. The friend I was renting from knew weeks in advance that I'd be moving out.

I received my training from a well-known nursing center located just one block away from one of the most respected hospitals in Orange County, Hoag Hospital. From one extreme to another, what happened to me personally just months after settling in at my mother's place was absolutely the most terrifying moment of my life.

Every day while in the hospital, I documented in my daily

planner note by note, page by page, results to the day I was discharged. Below you will find that detailed report of what happened to me, which I kept for my medical records. In closing, I made the decision to post this letter on Facebook because my family and friends around the United States and overseas were deeply concerned. This letter was also provided to my Primary Care Physician/Internist who told me, "Maybe you should go to Medical School to study?"

Dear Friends and Family,
    In case you were wondering, here is a detailed report of what happened to me. On a scary note, **December 4th 2014**, I was rushed to Saddleback Hospital Laguna Hills by ambulance to Critical Care Unit. I was at my Mother's condo at the time this occurred. My whole body was shaking with uncontrollable convulsions.
    The next morning, I was transferred to Hoag Hospital Irvine. Then one week after, I was transferred to Hoag Hospital Newport Beach where everything took place. **From December 4th 2014 to January 20th 2015,** I was hospitalized. Initially, what I thought was just a bad virus, derived in the summer of 2014. As months passed, my condition slowly turned out to progress for the WORSE. I caught a form of strep which triggered off a serious infection. A team of doctors diagnosed this as **Endo Bacterial Carditis.** This infection could have been stored in my body for quite some time and just creeped up out of nowhere.
    The team of doctors treating me all agreed this infection stemmed from a dentist's office. Furthermore, I most likely missed taking my antibiotics before having any dental procedure, including cleaning, because of my heart murmur. My symptoms were constant coughing, night sweats, body shakes and unexplained weight loss. I lost almost 30 pounds! I was scared.
    An Oncologist and an infectious disease doctor both told me that my white blood cells were highly elevated,

and they were very concerned. They explained to me that, because of this infection, my whole DNA got literally turned upside down! I had to have a pick line inserted in my right arm for two months of therapy with some pretty strong antibiotics. Ampicillin 500 mg and before that, Rocephin which worked but only so much. I had a tube camera jammed down my throat which was extremely uncomfortable, to detect any further findings. It clearly showed vegetation deposits that had formed and were eating away one of my four heart valves.

I was terrified when I heard this news. My mouth was so sore, I could hardly speak for a month! From that reading, it was inevitable what would happen next. On **January 12th 2015**, I had to undergo open heart surgery with a new heart valve placed and had a bypass performed from a blocked artery near my heart. Surgery took six hours!

I lost a lot of blood. The surgeon told me I would need a blood transfusion which I did not expect. Between a brain scan, an abdomen and spleen scan, an MRI, an EKG, a trans esophageal echocardiogram, and every blood test imaginable, they all came out negative. However, it was diagnosed from a bone marrow biopsy that I have **CML Leukemia Cancer**. The good news if any, is that this particular cancer is treatable and is getting closer to a cure within the next decade.

I have to take **Tasigna 150 mg** that's four pills a day for at least the next five years, with another two pills. **Metropolol 25 mg and baby aspirin 81 mg.** To top things off, the last problem, which might have stemmed from my initial infection, is the throbbing pain on my left shoulder cuff. For the past six months, I've periodically had to take Vicodin and Advil pills. My orthopedic surgeon sent me for six weeks of physical therapy. But still, pain comes and goes.

I had X-rays, which did not reveal anything unusual. However, my MRI with doctor's diagnosis, revealed **left**

shoulder edema mild Atrophy / Brachial Neuritis OR Radiculitis NOS. Unfortunately, I can only lift a ten-pound weight with my left arm but thirty-five pounds with my right arm. This will affect my job if I have to lift wine boxes for any given amount of time.

This November 2015, I have an appointment to see a well-known neurologist in Fountain Valley who just might be able to help me. Seriously, after what I have been through, I'm thinking about retiring early at sixty-two. I just turned sixty in July. I am hoping and praying things will work out.

Looking back, I enjoyed thirty-plus years in the music business, and I have been making a good living these past ten years in the wine and spirits industry. Still, my passion for music will never fade. Currently, I'm working only 6-12 hours a week, part-time as an independent contractor for a distributor in Napa Valley. The rest of the week, I'm a caregiver for my mother. As you may have heard, I had recently moved into her condominium. I do not have the energy to work a full-time 40 plus hour week any time soon.

In closing, I am feeling better now, but life will never be quite the same.

Andrew

One quick note: Just before being discharged from the hospital, the heart surgeon that performed my surgery checked my blood pressure and heart. He then smiled.

I asked him, "What are you smiling about, doctor?"

He told me, "Your heart murmur is gone!"

The fact is, when I was born my heart had an extra beat, so that was fantastic news! I was happy. Also, one of the staff doctors told me, "Andrew, you've worked in the music business for a while. Did you know singer Bobby Darin had a similar situation close to yours?

"In the 1970's, after he didn't take his antibiotics to protect his heart before his dental visit, Bobby developed sepsis. That's a very serious infection. He required two artificial heart valves. His case, of course, was much different than yours, and more complicated. Take care of yourself."

Shortly after that letter was written, believe it or not, I started working again. Only part-time. Can you imagine six months of not being able to work? I will admit, it felt strange at first and I did have my limitations. Doctors told me to just not pick up anything heavy. So, on Saturday May 15th 2015, with the help from my good friend David, and armed with twelve cases of wine, I participated in a large charity event with funds supporting music programs in South Bay Public Schools (pre schools, elementary and junior high) in Rolling Hills Estates, Palos Verdes, California. More than eighty people attended a night of Asian Fusion celebrating the year of the Sheep. In addition to pouring wine, I had to speak about each varietal in between each of the three main courses being served. Just picture me speaking to all these people on a microphone (think Howard Stern). My friend videotaped me cracking up.

Thinking back, it was unbelievable what I went through and, still, will never know how this infection even started.

♪♫♪

Months later, I received a phone call to participate in an unusual event, The Ultimate Women's Expo at Anaheim Convention Center, pouring wine at a designated booth. Turned out it was more like a Girls Gone Wild Expo. I had to take photos for the owner of the company as to what went on. One daring gal grabbed a bottle I was serving right off my table while I was getting more ice to fill in my ice bucket.

"Having fun while I can," she said.

"Are you?" I asked her. Then I had to take the bottle back from her. "I don't want you to get in trouble and get kicked outta here now, ya crazy nut!" I said.

She was drunk but good-looking. After it was all over, I was thinking what a cool gig I have. Best part-time job ever!

Well, moving on, I was a caregiver for my mother till the day she passed away at age ninety. That was on October 28th 2016. For those few years, I cooked, cleaned, administered her pills and drove her to her doctor's appointments. I had to sit her carefully on her wheelchair down a flight of nine stairs from her condo. That wasn't easy, as she had just had her left leg amputated! I'll never forget that phone call from her vascular doctor, who also was a surgeon, explaining to me that the only way to save my mother's life would be to amputate her left leg. This was extremely emotional for me, my brother, my sister and all our relatives.

On the day of surgery, my mother told me she just wanted to die. She had a hardening of the arteries and a severe blood clot, yet no diabetes.

Surgery took place in December 2015. On that very day I told her, "Mom, after this unexpected surgery, hopefully the last of your life, and this past year of events, all I can say is that you are the most courageous woman I have ever known. The angels above are praying for you, providing strength, as well as your children who love you so much. We cannot bear to let you leave this earth. Family and friends feel the same way. A new life awaits you. Things will be difficult, but the love and support we have for you is so strong. God has been watching over you in mysterious ways. In the years ahead, just remember, I will always be by your side."

Well, that is exactly what happened; my brother and I were right by her side for her very last breath and heartbeat. Just before she passed, something miraculous happened. Her eyes were closed that day, but she could still hear. As I held my hand over her forehead, her left eye opened for a couple of seconds looking straight at me! My brother witnessed this and was shocked, but in a good way. I then gently closed her eyelid and wept.

The next day I phoned her doctor and told him what had happened.

"That occurrence is uncommon but happens from time to time, usually right before people die," he told me. "In other words, it's their last glimpse of life.

He then said, "Your mother was saying goodbye to you and

that should make you very happy and proud."

Mother meant so much to so many. She was kind and loving, with arms always open to friends and family and anyone who entered her path. She painted, played piano, loved art and music. Even though her painting ceased, her love of music continued right until her very passing.

Not a day goes by without me thinking of her, especially when I brew coffee in the morning. She would always ask me, "Is the coffee ready yet?"

She preferred her coffee black, strong, smooth and rich, with no cream.

She's now with my father in spirit, floating on a fluffy cloud in heaven. I miss them both tremendously. Life has not been the same without them.

Well, at this stage of my life I made the decision to move away to a destination with less stress and more peace of mind. I sold Mother's condo and left Orange County. I had visited Palm Springs several times in the past and found it relaxing. I had often thought, maybe one day I'd reside there. So, as planned, at age sixty-two, I retired early to Palm Desert, California.

Remembering what my lawyer told me long ago, "You'll find another place and be okay."

Yep! I purchased another home with a pool and two Jacuzzis just steps away, high up in the mountains and centrally located. Every day is like summer, like I'm on a permanent vacation. I'll put it this way: Nice stop for me at this moment in time.

What does the future hold? I don't know! Not the slightest idea. I could possibly retire overseas in Belize or Portugal. Maybe Mexico or Spain. I'll just have to wait and see.

Hey! Wait a second! This book ain't over yet!

♪♫♪

So, the first thing I did after settling in was to contact a high-end audio and video home theater company in town. I visited two places before making my decision. The owner came over to my place with his tech crew to examine my situation.

He told me, "No wonder you phoned us! We haven't seen this much wiring and audio gear since we last looked in our own warehouse! You have quite a bit of stuff here, buddy!"

When technicians finished their work, almost three hours of correct configurations, I've gotta say I haven't heard music sound any better. As a matter of fact, when living by the beach in Dana Point, not only was my system setup incorrectly; I had less damn room to play with in my living room!

I couldn't believe that after all of these years, I was able to hear my audio-video surround sound system the way it should sound. It felt like I was in a professional recording studio. No lie! Honestly, I was overwhelmed with joy. From that day on, I've been making up for all that lost time by playing my music. Once again, no neighbor's above or below me! And it gets even better. Turns out, the couple next door to me are Canadian Snowbirds, so they're gone many months out of the year! Things are perfectly placed and my whole house is filled with music in every room. My desktop computer is loaded up with tons of tunes and my new Pro Media 2.1 THX certified computer speakers and sub-woofer sound *Sick!* In my bedroom, I have another stereo with added subwoofer, even my HE washer and dryer in the laundry room play a little musical ditty after washing cycle is done!

So, after residing in the desert for one year, I decided to rent my spare bedroom and bath out to a student since the local college is just two-and-a-half miles away. This is where things really get nuts.

I placed a local ad on Craigslist and answered an ad on Craigslist. The latter of the two resulted in an appointment between me and other party. All I knew was that this girl was a college student seeking a room near her work and school. Upon meeting her, the first thing she said to me when entering my residence was, "Wow! Your place reminds me of my stepdad's home." Considering hanging on the walls in my living room are Frank Sinatra, Jimi Hendrix, The Beatles and a few vintage movie posters, I asked, "Who the heck is your Stepdad?

She said, "Terry Reid."

I told her to wait a second. Then pulled out a record from my collection, *Bang, Bang You're Terry Reid*, his debut LP on Epic Records from 1968. She pointed him out immediately on front cover. Terry was only nineteen years old when that LP came out! When she recognized him so quickly, I knew this just had to be true. So, how does something like this fall into my lap? I'll never know, nor understand.

I asked her, "How come you don't have an English accent?

She said, "He's my stepdad, silly!"

Oh, yeah, sorry. I was hesitant to write about this story in my book, but just had to as this just doesn't happen to many people. Besides, I want everyone to know about what an incredible vocalist/songwriter Terry is. I just wish he'd get the recognition he richly deserves and that is way overdue. He's a brilliant guitarist as well. His songs have been covered by dozens of artists such as Cheap Trick, John Mellencamp and The Raconteurs, and he still tours! Well, we talked about arrangements and what her needs would be. I wanted her to be comfortable. She then moved in.

On a side note, it's interesting to note how many rock stars and celebrities reside here in the desert. Vocalists Paul Rodgers and Mickey Thomas from Jefferson Starship; I found that amusing. Mickey and his wife opened a new Bowl of Heaven Smoothies and Juice Bar from their growing franchise here in Palm Desert. Actor Gary Oldman recently purchased a home in Palm Springs. Actors Kurt Russell and Goldie Hawn own a huge mansion directly across the street from where I live. Queens of the Stone Age are from here as well. More recently, just a few miles away from my place, Gerald Casale, of Devo fame, listed his home in Palm Desert for one-and-a-half million dollars. Guess you never know who your neighbor might be? But I suppose you all know the deep, rich history of Palm Springs, from entertainers like Bing Crosby to Frank Sinatra, who owned property here in the 1950's –1960's and so on.

After a few months passed, Terry's stepdaughter decided to invite her parents over for dinner. She told me they were both picky eaters. But she knew I was a good cook. I didn't want to fuck this up and, I will admit, I was a bit nervous. I had stored an expensive 1.5 liter of wine in my wine cooler for a special occasion. I guessed this was a good time to uncork that baby. She also warned me not to mention the connection between Led Zeppelin and Terry. I promised and, believe me, I knew all about that whole story after reading many articles in magazines and so forth. It's a pretty sensitive subject. However, just so you know, Robert Plant and Jimmy Page are friends with Terry to this very day.

The meal I prepared was a large piece of king salmon drizzled on top with sweet ginger teriyaki marinade and the juice of half of a fresh, sweet tangerine, and finally drizzled with extra virgin olive oil with a dash of freshly ground black pepper. When done, I took it out of the oven and served it on top of jasmine rice from Mali, Thailand.

The wine was chilled at a perfect 57 degrees. Right from the start, her parents said something smells really good, and when they tasted it, they said it was delicious. They enjoyed the wine so much that the three of us finished it off rather quickly. I had just a few bottles left in my cooler, so I picked out another perfect blend to pair up with the meal. I was thinking to myself, "Thank God, this all worked out."

I sat in the dining room chatting with Terry while mother and daughter sat in the living room catching up on things. We both shared our life stories, and he knew exactly what I was talking about as our age difference was only six years. I was taken by the fact that one of his best friends was Keith Richards, having grown up together in England. Keith looked out after Terry when he was, like, in his early teens. Funny, I'd think it would be the other way around?

I had many questions for Terry, such as what it was like to tour with The Beatles and The Stones, and what it was like meeting Hendrix. I asked him if he was friends with or knew many of the British bands on the scene in the 60's and '70's. Well, it turns out that he was friends with all my favorite bands from England. We spent the evening drinking, laughing and having a grand time.

I gave him a quick tour of my place and showed him my record collection, including rare vintage picture sleeve 45s. He flipped when looking through one of my cases because everything was set up alphabetically. First record he pulled out was The Animals. He laughed and said, "Look at Eric Burdon, he looks like a little kid!"

Then told me he's good friends with Eric and that he lived in Joshua Tree for a while, then moved to Idyllwild, a small town in the Southern California mountains, about an hour's ride from where I reside.

He was looking through the Beatles, Badfinger, Dave Clark Five, then stopped and yelled for his wife, "Honey! You've got to see this!"

It was a Hayley Mills 45 rpm with picture sleeve "Jeepers Creepers" on Buena Vista Records from 1962. He knew her too! Guess they were neighbors back in England. I swear, it was like going through the history of rock and roll. As the night progressed, I wanted Terry to hear his debut album (as mentioned above) on my stereo. The big question I asked him was, "How does this record sound compared to when you were in the studio recording?"

To my dismay he said, "There's something wrong here. Hold on."

He then moved my subwoofer over in between my front right speaker, and asked me if my back speakers could be adjusted. I told him, "Hell, yeah!"

So, I turned the dials up on both rear speakers. Sure enough, we could hear more bottom bass from the two subwoofers built into my speakers. It did sound better!

He smiled and said, "There ya go."

Then I did something by switching the setting on my preamp, right then and there. He said, "This is pretty close to how things sounded back then," and added, "See? that's all ya needed to do. Just a little rearranging with a master's touch."

When leaving my place, Terry hugged me and his wife said, "Thanks for taking care of my daughter."

Next morning, his stepdaughter told me she'd received a text from her mom about how much fun she had, that the food was delicious and that her parents loved me. I felt so happy and honored to have met them both.

It was a night I'll never forget.

♪ ♪♪ ♪

Living in the desert, I've visited many cool places. Every other weekend, I'll take a quick trip to Palm Springs to check out the scene. There's a place to pick up freshly baked bagels and pastries that a few people had told me about when I conducted wine tastings in town. They were from New York and San Francisco, so I figured it must be a Jewish Deli. Stopped by one day to see for myself. The place is called Townie Bagels Bakery Café. There was a line outside, so I figured it must be a popular spot. I told the owner they tasted close to New York style. He told me he was originally from New York and said they used old school methods, where the bagels are mixed and shaped upside down for a couple of minutes, then flipped over and baked till golden brown. Gee, is that why they tasted so good and flavorful? Anyway, just two blocks away from Townie's I found many antique and mid-century modern shops to visit.

On the corner, I noticed an unusual place. It looked like an old shack in disrepair. When I got closer, I noticed many Jimi Hendrix posters and black-and-white photo strips covering the front windows that miraculously I had never seen before. The place was named, Michael McGarry's AAA Palm Stars. *What an odd name*, I thought. I just had to walk in and find out what this was all about. When entering this tiny shop, I noticed most of the items were Native American and cowboy artifacts and collectibles. In the middle of the store sat a long table with a load of B&W vintage photos of Hollywood celebrities in many wooden boxes. As I was sorting through, what stunned me was a box containing over two hundred photos of the Jimi Hendrix Experience. According to the owner, they were taken around 1968–1969, when he visited Beverly Hills, California. He told me many shots were taken at the Beverly Hills Hotel during their 1969 US Tour just weeks before the Hendrix Experience broke up, and a few months before Jimi played at Woodstock.

"How in the world did you acquire these photos?" I asked him.

The owner of shop told me that Alan Pappé was the photographer who took these rare photos. That day when I got home, I searched on the web and was surprised that Alan Pappé had worked for every major motion picture studio, including Columbia Pictures, Universal, MGM, Warner Bros, 20th Century and Paramount. He had photographed countless celebrities within the music and film industry of the 1960's and 1970's: Sharon Tate, Barbara Streisand, Brooke Shields, Al Pacino, and Buffalo Springfield, to name a few. He shot the memorable front album cover of *Grease* with John Travolta and Olivia Newton John. Lastly, his portrait of Liza Minnelli in the film *Cabaret* was on the front cover of both Time magazine and Newsweek, earning him special recognition.

The owner of shop told me this renowned photographer left all his negatives to his sister before he passed away in 2008. The owner of the shop had an exclusive arrangement with the estate. All the negatives are now in his hands! Unbelievable that I've actually seen only a few of these photographs on the Internet.

As I was leaving, he told me, if I wanted, he could print up photos of interest. But of course, for a price, but he did say he'd work with me. Seriously, I'm saving up money as I speak. I have to say, it was pretty exciting to see all these unseen photos from fifty years ago.

So, here I am in 2018. It's mid-October now. After all the years that have passed, I figured it's time to purchase another guitar and amplifier, as the urge for me to play again reached tremendous heights.

I searched many musical instrument websites for weeks looking for a Gibson Les Paul similar to my old one, and a small practice amp, preferably Fender, to play at home and record with whenever needed. Sounds simple, right? Not nearly. I was quite shocked that my old Les Paul was selling for at least $5,500 and upwards to $9,000!

Yeah, shocked but not surprised. I just about gave up. But I figured where there is a will, there is a way. So, I kept on looking, with no luck. I was astonished that later Les Paul's were so damn expensive. Just by chance, I stumbled on a first production Les Paul Studio 60's Tribute with 2 P 90 pickups from 2011. There were five Colorways offered back then: Worn Gold Top, Worn Honey Burst, Worn Heritage Cherry Burst, Worn Ebony and Worn White. They looked cool and had that vintage look. Thought maybe this could work out as they looked similar to my old 1955 Les Paul Junior.

I was told by my musician friends that in 2011, when first reissued, this Les Paul was built better than the current production models put out in 2012, as it featured a one-piece Rosewood fretboard. Gibson went to baked maple fingerboards in 2012, which robbed you of that vintage tone. Only thing I was concerned about was that the body did not have that glossy, polished look. It was priced to sell back in the day because of a few alterations, such as a satin finish which could get chipped easily. With that said, I looked carefully again and found a beautiful Cherry Sunburst on eBay, of all places. It was seriously the best-looking color out of all five. It was supposedly locked up in a closet and the seller hardly ever played it.

I knew I was taking a huge risk, not playing it in person, but took the chance and ordered it. When delivered, it played okay, but felt nothing even close to my old 55". Put on new strings, polished it up and played for a few months, but this Les Paul did not have that smooth feeling I had from my previous guitar.

Sadly, I decided it had to go. Sold it for a small profit and moved on. Oh, the amplifier! Let's not even go there. So, is there a moral to this story? Yep. I'll need to search again for that perfect guitar and amplifier, but this time, moving forward, I will play it in person. I'm a real sucker for vintage equipment, so it'll take a long while from now to afford the guitar that is right for me.

It is now July 2019 and my sixty-fourth birthday is right around the corner. It's been three years now that I've been living in the desert. Am I getting used to the different weather? Well, yes and no. I'm not really accustomed to these summer months when the temperature rises to 118 degrees. From May to the end of September, it pretty much stays *Hot*.

Other than that, it's a nice, easy-going place to reside. From October to April, we have more pleasant weather. So, these days you can pretty much find me on social media posting write-ups on important and familiar music acts of the day. Finally, in my life of semi-retirement, I'm now having the time to search through the thousands of vinyl LP's and compact disc's in my music library to listen to and enjoy.

Now, here are a few interesting and fascinating facts I've learned during these past few years. What I've been notic-ing more and more of in this new millennium are these 50th Anniversary Box Sets commemorating iconic classic albums being released. They include many formats such as a Special Blu-ray disc in 5.1 DTS HD Surround Sound. Also, 180-220-gram remastered vinyl LP's and unreleased and alternate recordings from the same album. There's also a format called SACD (Super Audio CD) which was introduced officially in 1999. It was devel-oped by Sony and Philips Electronics and intended to be a huge upgrade to the compact disc format. It also offers more audio channels, a higher bit rate and longer playing time than a con-ventional CD. However, you'll have to own an SACD player or a DVD player with their logo stamped on front panel.

Through the years to this very day, not many titles have been produced either. But a few fine examples of exceptional recordings are The Allman Brothers' *Live at Fillmore East,* The Moody Blues Catalog, Pink Floyd's - *Dark Side of the Moon,* and most recently King Crimson's *In the Court of the Crimson King* and The Rolling Stones' *Let It Bleed* 50th Anniversary Box set, including vinyl LP's with SACD's in Mono and Stereo.

Well, these past few years I just had to purchase The Beatles' *Sgt. Pepper, The White Album,* and *Abbey Road.* All have been reissued with a boatload of extras: unreleased songs, demos, a book with unpublished photographs, and an added Blu-ray 5.1 recording remastered, plus other gems marking their 50th anniversary.

Can you imagine listening to The Beatles in surround sound? This is something I never expected nor even dreamed of till now. This seems to be the future of new technology coming forward, but I can't really predict for sure. Owning quite a few of these sets, I do have to say listening to them in a multi-channeled format is something special. Best I've heard thus far is DTS (Digital Theater Sound) in surround sound.

When Jimi Hendrix's *Electric Ladyland* was released, and even though I own multiple formats from the first pressing on vinyl, I just had to purchase. It was the first limited edition box set that I acquired. That also started my new obsession in collecting, and from that day on I was hooked. I'll literally go broke if this keeps on happening, and I truly think this trend will never end. Here are just a few reviews of mine you need to read to understand this new format in sound:

Hello Everyone!

On August 1st 1968, Jeff Beck's "TRUTH" was released. Gotta say owning multiple versions Import and Domestic including 1st pressing on LP, in my opinion the best sound quality by far is This limited numbered edition from Audio Fidelity. Jeff Beck -Truth. Hybrid/SACD. AFZ-269 #1200 of 5000 pressed Worldwide.

When I originally found out about this special pressing in 2017, I phoned Audio Fidelity directly and spoke to President Marshall Blonstein. He told me it was already Sold Out, but would hold me a copy he had on his desk. To my sadness, it was actually held for some Record Executive. I was angry especially, since I knew Marshall from years back when He owned DCC Compact Classics.

Original price was $29.99. Since that being the case, had to purchase on Fucking eBay. Was pretty lucky to get for $35.00 and all considering, well worth it. Just for kicks look it up on eBay. It's currently going upwards to $500.00! One of my favorite Albums of All time!

With that said, which format sounds the best? Well, without a doubt This SACD Rules! It sounded as close as to actually being in the Recording Studio. Every instrument, electric bass, electric & acoustic guitars, drums, tympani, organ, piano & bagpipes were Distinctly more pronounced.

Rod Stewart's vocals were absolutely perfect! He never sounded better giving a powerful punch to this Iconic heavy blues rock recording. Jeff Beck's guitar work was outstanding. Loved his messin around with that wah wah pedal to perfection. Ron Wood played bass back then. As a matter of fact, think he's a better bass player than guitarist. It definitely shows on this album.

The great Nicky Hopkins played some killer piano & John Paul Jones (Pre -Zeppelin) added Hammond Organ on "Ol Man River. Even Jimmy Page played 12 string guitar on "Beck's Bolero" but was not credited as well as Keith Moon who played drums on that same song! There are sometimes record contracts that prevent these things from happening.

Other thing I wondered about was Mick Waller. He in my opinion was a pretty solid drummer, but thought there could have been a better choice on this recording. Wish it was Keith Moon? LOL.

Well, moving on, this SACD sounded crisp and clean and imaged Beautifully. You could clearly hear Jimmy Page's 12 string acoustic guitar on Beck's Bolero. After entire disc ended, my ears were ringing. It was like being at an actual live concert! I did have it on loud close to 100+ decibels. But seriously, this recording from 1968 produced by Mickey Most was like listening to it for the first time.

Stunning job by Steve Hoffman and Steven Marsh at Marsh Mastering. The Original recording had too much hiss. This cleaned up Masterpiece had more bottom (Bass & Drums). Honestly, every nuance sounded so much richer & full bodied. Accuracy & Clarity simply amazing.

In closing, you really have to own Hi End audio equipment to hear what has actually been achieved. The audio gear used was my Delphi Imager Speakers. The imaging full dimensional sound they produce delivers 3-dimensional True Stereo coupled with astounding dynamics. Only other speaker used was my Definitive Technology Powerfied Subwoofer. Just 3 Speakers!

Dear friends, if you can find this SACD for a decent price, You Seriously need for your collection. Trust me!

Here's my 2nd review:

Hello Friends,

It's Sunday and living here in the desert an unusual 63 degrees with heavy gusty winds up here, high in the mountains. Looked outside and noticed palm tree bark spread all over the place! So, what better day than to play music? Many of you are, without a doubt, familiar with Neil Young's album *Harvest* from 1972. Well, what you may not know is that in 2002, DTS Audio released, for the 30th anniversary of *Harvest*, a limited-edition, multi-channel recording, enhancing the original album's production with mixes designed specifically for this DVD audio.

Years later, I found a copy in a used bin for five dollars. I forgot which record store. Although the cover was beaten-up, the disc was in immaculate condition. I just played it with my new upgraded equipment and was stunned how amazing this recording sounded in surround sound and eight speakers. As a matter of fact, I never played it till now. Remarkable sounding, full-bodied masterpiece! Honestly, I felt like I was in the studio while Neil was recording it. Crisp, clear refined vocals; instrumentation like I never ever heard before! Sounded completely different than the conventional LP.

Well, there ya have it! I'm filled with joy. Best five dollars I've ever spent. I checked out eBay and since it's now deleted, it's going for over $100.00!! Yikes!

Here's my last review:

Dear Friends,

First off, if you do not own a SACD player or own any other audio equipment that has the icon on equipment used, then you will not be able to get the full insane effect of multi-channel madness. You'll only be able to hear in stereo and in some rare cases, this disc may not play at all.

So, today in the mail I just received my copy of Pink Floyd's Dark Side SACD that I never knew existed until I read an article about a month ago on how amazing it sounded. I did some research and found it came out in 2003 and has since been long out of print. Checked eBay last week to discover prices ranging in good condition from $35–$125. Well, I found a perfect copy but had to shell out $41.51. That's almost three times the original price.

Nevertheless, no regrets whatsoever. Pink Floyd's The Dark Side of The Moon 30th Anniversary Limited Edition 5.1 Surround Mix SACD-Digital Remaster Capitol/EMI CDP 7243 S 82136 2-1US.

Upon initial listen, it was like hearing this album for the first time in a different dimension, different world. I completely freaked out and was lost in outer space! Goodness gracious, I was in complete awe of what I had been missing out on all these years. Honestly, there were sounds, voices, creeping up behind me with rear speakers, while all instrumentation spread out all over my living room, with three subwoofers pounding deep heavy bass. It was like sitting in a huge theater!

I'll need to invite you all over some day to witness the experience I just had. When Pink Floyd was in the studio, working with Alan Parsons decades ago on the Quadrophonic mixes. The vinyl pressing was a matrix 4 channel recording. This disc was partially taken from those tapes. However, magnified a billion times over to a whole new level in sound. Basically, unlike anything you have ever heard before! Recorded originally in 1972–1973, I was shocked—but in a good way. All vocals were coming out of my center channel while all keyboards and synthesizers spread out imaging from front to rear speakers.

By the way, I have eight speakers in my total setup.

The song "Time" blew me away as I heard all clocks and bells in surround sound mania! Wow! And I played it pretty Loud! Double Wow! Front subwoofer and two rear subwoofers brought more depth and fullness to this recording. I also played it in stereo. It sounded fine, but when switching back to SACD mode, Holy shit!!!

Well, there ya have it. Just so you know, I own the original pressing on LP. And then in September of 1992, for Pink Floyd's 20th Anniversary, I had to purchase the Digitally Remastered CD Box. The 20th Anniversary pressing was quite impressive, but in no way close to this SACD recording. Just wish these record labels would quit pressing up all these multiple formats and quit messing around with the original recordings and just let things be. Guess with all the Digital, Super Mega Hi Technology available today, it will never stop.

So, as to my life in music, here is some news that I found amusing. It's also kind of a funny way to end this book. On September 6th, 2019, Rolling Stone magazine published an article that mentioned vinyl is poised to outsell CDs for the first time since 1986, and that in the near future the revenue generated by record sales is likely to surpass the revenue generated by CD.

Sales of vinyl records have enjoyed constant growth in recent years. At the same time, CD sales have taken a nosedive. Last year the RIAA (Recording Industry Association of America) mid-year report suggested that CD sales were declining three times as fast as vinyl sales were growing.

What does that tell you? Nothing you don't already know really. In today's world, I still play vinyl, CD, SACD, Blu-ray discs, even a few vintage laser discs I have laying around I play every so often.

Getting back to vinyl records, they are tangible and have this certain appeal as to buying something and being able to physically handle it. New millennial buyers are more likely to regard their purchase as something of value when it's a physical object than something they just downloaded.

Back in the day, and even today, the extra bonus of a poster inserted in record jacket was a cool thing to experience that you can't get in a CD 5" format.

Thinking back, when I was a kid growing up, I remember hanging those posters up on my bedroom wall. Beatles and Pink Floyd, for example. Colored vinyl is another aspect, as well as picture discs. Back in 1931 when RCA Victor first introduced this format of vinyl plastic long playing record, they were designed to play at 33 1/3. The music contained about ten minutes per side. Then years later, it was advanced to get more information in the groove. Before all that, in the 1930's, 78's were introduced. My grandparents had quite an impressive collection stored in their RCA

Victor console cabinet that I vividly remember.

So, there we go. back to the basics.

As this book closes, it is undeniable that music is universal and makes the world go round. It certainly did mine.

Music brings up many emotions of love, serenity, happiness, anger and sadness. To me, a day without music is like a day without sunshine.

Dear readers, with deep appreciation, I'd like to thank each and every one of you for taking this roller-coaster of a journey with me through memories happy and sad. God bless the doctors that saved my life. I'm proud to say, I'm now cancer-free and feel much healthier than I've felt in many years.

A new life-phase awaits. Let's just hope it's worth waiting for.

Peace and Love to You All,
Andrew.

Acknowledgments

I must acknowledge the holy spirits of my grandparents and my mother and father in Heaven that channeled me spiritually to write this book about my life in music that started with me from the day I was born.

Grandpa Sam's Drug Store 1926

Grandma and me in 1958

My Mom & Dad on vacation in the 1950s

Me as Popeye 1960

Killer Kane Band photo by William Forney 1976

Motor City Bad Boys Need Help Fast

Motor City Bad Boys Detroit Free Press article 1975

BY CHRISTINE BROWN
Free Press Staff Writer

The debut of the Motor City Bad Boys was something like the old pink Cadillac that serves as a platform for their drummer: It appeared to have all the right elements until you inspected a bit further and found out it was only half there.

The Bad Boys are five (sometimes six musicians—two from New York and the rest from Detroit—who have been working for a year and a half toward becoming Detroit's newest contribution to punk rock.

None had extensive musical experience, and they spent the last six months writing songs and making tapes that were circulated to record companies.

Wednesday night they made their live debut at the Latin Quarter, and no place could have been more appropriate. The Latin Quarter is a rather tacky old 'club on

Grand Blvd., a block east of Woodward, and everything there is just a bit tawdry, just a bit garish like the overdone paintings that hang over the bar.

WHAT BETTER place for the debut of a band which proved itself worthier of the "Bad" part of its name than of the "Motor City" connection?

It's quite possible the Motor City Bad Boys will be big, rich and successful some day, per-

The Boys sound like the Indianapolis 500

haps in the near future. The band seems to have borrowed bits of Kiss, Alice Cooper, Iggy Stooge and others, and if those groups can make the big time, so can the Bad Boys.

Drummer Spence Spencer, guitarists Billy Wimble and Andy Jay, and bass player Rick Lockhart obviously know their way around their instruments. But their songs so totally lack variety that the band's problems but insisted the weak spots could be overcome in just two or three weeks.

The chief problem of the Bad Boys at this point is unfortunately the most visible: lead singer Sirius Trixon, who mumbles his way through lyrics.

With stringy hair, dark

But success requires a combination of luck, talent and hard work, and it's not yet clear just how much of all that the Bad Boys are dealing with.

The band is strong instrumentally—so powerful, in fact, that you could believe the Indy 500 was taking place during their debut.

Trixon's chief problem seems to be working with crowds. When a few people got up to do what the Bad Boys beat urges—dance—planned they had been Trixon became hysterical, cursing those who dare dance while he was shouting his songs.

The day after the Bad Boys' less-than-stunning premiere, Joel Solaka, one of the group's managers, acknowledged the

hairy underarms, a slightly pudgy body and a completion problem, Trixon is not the most appealing lead singer.

"I'm going to hire a voice coach for Sirius," Solaka said. "He needs to learn to enunciate. Billy and Andy can sing, too, and we're going to have them on a few numbers."

Solaka is associated with Showline Productions, which promoted concerts in the Detroit area a few years ago. His promotional talents have been turned toward boosting the Bad Boys, and some record and rock media people at the Latin Quarter debut combined they had been "hyped" into coming with promises that Alice Cooper (who was performing in Knoxville) would be there and that a lavish buffet would be provided (sandwiches were $1.50).

Even so, Arista and MCA are apparently interested in the Bad Boys for a record deal, Solaka said, if the problems can be eliminated.

The question that remains is whether the "Bad" in the band's name will come to mean good, raunchy rock, or whether it will continue to be taken literally.

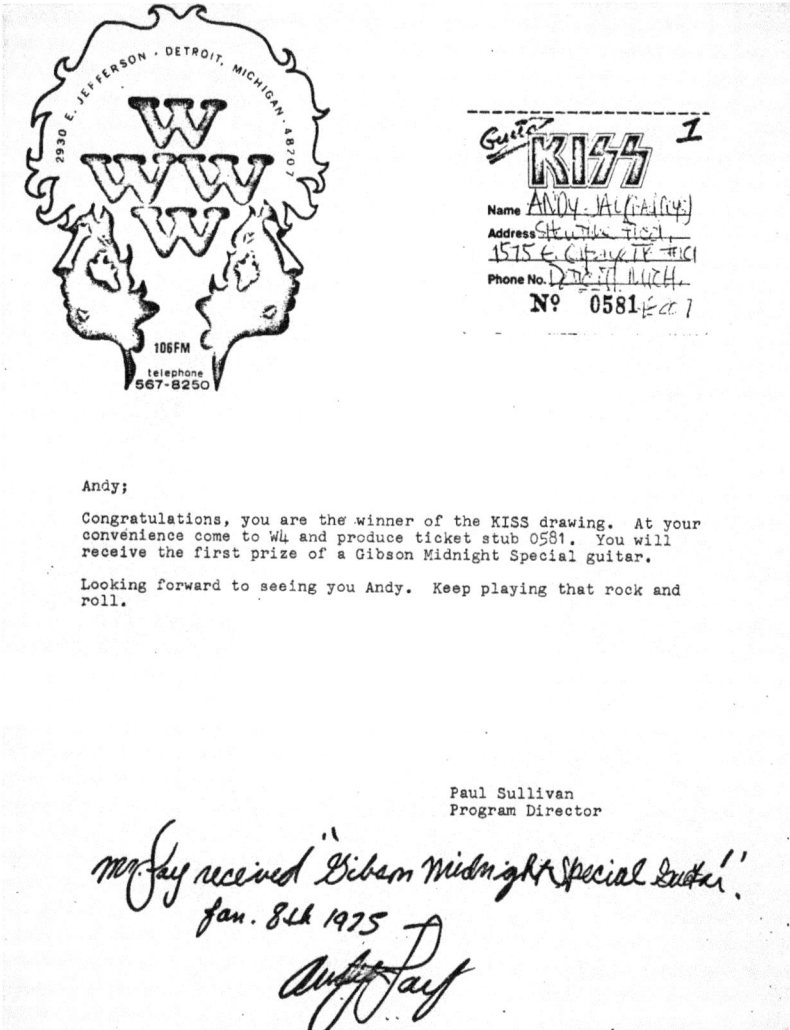

Andy;

Congratulations, you are the winner of the KISS drawing. At your convenience come to W4 and produce ticket stub 0581. You will receive the first prize of a Gibson Midnight Special guitar.

Looking forward to seeing you Andy. Keep playing that rock and roll.

Paul Sullivan
Program Director

WWW 106 FM Detroit, MI - KISS Contest 1975

Brother Kenny, Arthur, Blackie & me 1976 Starwood Club

Killer Kane, Rodney & me 1976 backstage Starwood Club

Robert Fripp (King Crimson), Randy & me and WEA
warehouse manager Dick White 1981

www.ingramcontent.com/pod-product-compliance
Lightning Source LLC
Chambersburg PA
CBHW031939090426
42811CB00002B/237